Equipping
The Believer

Equipping
The Believer

David Corbin

Winchester, UK
Washington, USA

First published by Circle Books, 2013
Circle Books is an imprint of John Hunt Publishing Ltd., Laurel House, Station Approach,
Alresford, Hants, SO24 9JH, UK
office1@jhpbooks.net
www.johnhuntpublishing.com
www.circle-books.com

For distributor details and how to order please visit the 'Ordering' section on our website.

Text copyright: David Corbin 2012

ISBN: 978 1 78099 996 8

A CIP catalogue record for this book is available from the British Library.

Design: Stuart Davies

Printed in the USA by Edwards Brothers Malloy

We operate a distinctive and ethical publishing philosophy in all
areas of our business, from our global network of authors to
production and worldwide distribution.

CONTENTS

Acknowledgements

I want to thank God, who through the Holy Spirit, inspired me to write this book, and gave me the topics and words for the common good and the building up of other believers today, being our final authority in all matters pertaining to doctrine, reproof, correction, and instruction in righteousness (2 Tim. 3:16-17).

I would like to express my gratitude to my father, Rev. Bob van der Berg, who has shared his wealth of knowledge gained from serving the Lord in ministry, and who reviewed this book to confirm that I have understood the prompting of the Holy Spirit correctly in proclaiming the truth of the Gospel, as well as offered insights and comments.

I would also like to thank my wife, Letitia Corbin, for her support and continuous encouragement whilst researching and writing this book, as well as her commitment to me in understanding the precepts of God's Word.

David J. Corbin

Introduction

Many people have theories and opinions, and form doctrines as to what you as a believer need to do to please God. As a result, what we hear is not always what the Word of God says. This has caused much division amongst the Body of Christ. Some people will quote a scripture and put their own interpretation on it. But that is not how we as believers can best equip ourselves.

This book will provide you with an insight to your questions by looking at the Bible to see what the scriptures have to say. Use the Word of God as your basis, and everything that you hear or read needs to line up with the Word of God; otherwise it is merely someone's opinion and interpretation. Let the Bible interpret itself by cross referencing to other scriptures. You cannot build a doctrine on just one verse. The Bible says "...by the mouth of two or three witnesses the matter shall be established" (Deut. 19:15; Matt. 18:16; 2 Cor. 13:1).

My prayer is that the Holy Spirit will give you wisdom, knowledge and understanding as you read this book, to discern the truth, and find the answers and direction for your divine purpose in the Body of Christ.

This book is not copyright protected, as the content is God-inspired. Therefore, use this book, or portions thereof, and distribute it to equip like-minded men and women; teaching spiritual truths, imparting biblical knowledge, and grounding them in the message of God's unconditional love and grace.

Chapter I

Every Believer has Faith

1.1 Introduction

Faith is the most important subject in the Bible, and one of the fundamentals of Christianity, yet the least taught by the Church today and therefore the least understood and exercised subject by the believer. You cannot be saved without faith, because "...by grace you have been saved through faith..." (Eph. 2:8), neither can you live without faith nor please God without faith, because the Bible says "(F)or we walk by faith, not by sight" (2 Cor. 5:7), and "...without faith it is impossible to please Him..." (Heb. 11:6).

Furthermore, the Bible warns us that we are in a spiritual battle (Eph. 6:12). This battle is being fought in our minds, and not against flesh and blood; and it is only with faith that we are meant to overcome Satan's 'strongholds' and "(F)ight the good fight of faith..." (1 Tim. 6:12).

1.2 God Kind of Faith

Faith is our positive response to what God has already done for us. It is our response to His grace. It is not what we must do to make the Lord act on our behalf, but rather our response to what He has already done. In its simplicity, that is faith. From Scripture we see that there are two kinds of faith – the Thomas-like faith (or 'head' faith), and the Abraham-like faith (or 'heart' faith). The Thomas-like faith is inherent within every human being, whilst the Abraham-like faith is a supernatural faith that only comes to those who receive the good news.

After Jesus' resurrection, Jesus appeared to the disciples, "(N)ow Thomas...was not with them when Jesus came. The other disciples therefore said to him, 'We have seen the Lord'. So he said to them, 'Unless I see in His hands the print of the nails, and put my finger into the print of the nails, and put my hand into His side, I will not believe'" (John 20:24-25). Several days later, whilst the disciples were gathered together in a room, Jesus again appeared in their midst, and He said to Thomas, "...(R)each your finger here, and look at My hands; and reach your hand here, and put it into My side. Do not be unbelieving, but believing" (John 20:27). Jesus knew what Thomas had said even though He was not physically present that day when Thomas said it. We read on in John 20:28 that Thomas acknowledged Jesus as "My Lord and my God", and Jesus said to him, "...Thomas, because you have seen Me, you have believed. Blessed are those who have not seen and yet have believed" (John 20:29).

The Thomas-like faith can only believe what it can see, taste, hear, smell, or feel; it is limited to our five senses. Using this kind of faith, we can fly in aeroplanes when we do not fully understand how flying works, nor do we assess the pilot's credentials before boarding the aeroplane, but we trust that the flight will be okay. That is 'head' faith, which God gave to every person. What if I asked you to board an aeroplane that was missing one of its wings? You would not board that aeroplane even if you were offered bags of money to do so. Your physical senses would forbid it. In the same manner, Jesus did not commend Thomas' kind of faith. That is believing what your senses tell your mind; and everybody, believer and non-believer, has that kind of faith. Rather, Jesus said "...(B)lessed are those who have not seen and yet have believed" (John 20:29). This is the Abraham-kind of faith, which believes in spite of what our physical senses can perceive, or our circumstances can portray.

Man is a spirit being. He has a soul, and he lives in a body. Therefore, the Abraham-like faith is of the heart, or the spirit, or the inward man. Faith is not of the mind or the body, it is of the heart. The Bible reaffirms this through the following scripture: "...whoever says to this mountain, 'Be removed and be cast into the sea', and does not doubt in his **heart**..." (Mark 11:23) (emphasis mine). Similarly, in Prov. 3:5 it says, "Trust in the Lord with all your **heart**, and lean not on your own understanding" (emphasis mine).

1.3 God's Supernatural Faith

Look at Rom. 4:17, it says, "...God... calls those things which do not exist as though they did". God's faith goes beyond our physical senses. God's faith operates supernaturally, beyond the limitations of our 'head' faith. The context of this verse from Romans speaks about how God supernaturally blessed Abram and Sarai with a child in their old age. Abram was 100 and Sarai was 91 when Isaac was born. The year before Isaac's birth, when Abram still did not have a child by his wife, God told them the child was coming, and He changed Abram's name to Abraham and Sarai's name to Sarah. Abram meant 'high father', but Abraham means 'to be populous, father of a multitude'. God changed Abram's name and called him the father of a multitude before it came to pass. Rom. 4:17 explains this action by stating that "...God... calls those things which do not exist as though they did".

When the Lord created the universe, Gen. 1:3 tells us that He created light on the first day but did not create the sun, moon, and stars until the fourth day of creation (Gen. 1:14-19). The Lord called light into being first, and four days later created a source for the light to come from. That is not the way natural man does things. We are limited, but God calls things that are not as though they were. That is supernatural. Luke 18:27 reminds us that "...the things which are impossible with men are possible with God".

This supernatural faith is also the kind of faith we use to receive salvation. We have to believe in God, whom we have not seen, and believe that our sins are forgiven, which we cannot prove by natural means. It takes God's supernatural faith for us to receive salvation, and this supernatural faith comes from God's Word. Rom. 10:17 says "(S)o then faith comes by hearing, and hearing by the word of God". We access God's faith through His Word, and His Word always achieves that which it is meant to accomplish (Isa. 55:11). Once we receive God's supernatural faith at salvation, it does not leave us, according to Rom.11:29: "(F)or the gifts and the calling of God are irrevocable". The instant we are saved, a change occurs within our heart, or spirit, or our inward man. We receive a new spirit and our new spirit becomes one with God's Spirit (1 Cor. 6:17). The Holy Spirit constantly produces faith (Gal. 5:22), therefore, within our new spirit is all the faith we will ever need (Col. 2:10).

The same faith that God used to create the worlds in the beginning is a permanent part of our born-again spirit. Yet there are believers praying for more faith. Mark 11:23 says "(F)or assuredly, I say to you, whoever says to this mountain, 'Be removed and be cast into the sea', and does not doubt in his heart, but believes that those things he says will be done, he will have whatever he says'". This faith that Jesus is talking about is the God-kind of faith, or God's supernatural faith, or the Abraham-kind of faith; and every believer already has the measure of this kind of faith. You do not have to search for it; you do not have to pray for it; you do not have to fast for it; and you do not have to promise to do greater and better works to get it. You already have it! "...God hath dealt to every man the measure of faith" (Rom. 12:3, KJV). God did not give us different measures of faith; we all received THE measure of faith. If I were serving soup to a group of people, and if I used the same serving spoon to dish it out, then that serving spoon would be THE measure. Everyone would get the same amount of soup because I would use the same measure. That is the way it is with God's supernatural faith. He only used one measure. Paul reminds us in Rom. 2:11 that "...there is no partiality with God". All born-again Christians received the same amount of faith. There is just a lack of knowing and using what God has already given us.

1.4 Faith is Substance

Many believers think faith is acting like something has happened when in reality it has not, and if we imagine this for long enough, then it will come to pass. But that is not what faith is. According to Heb. 11:1 the Bible says that "(N)ow faith is the substance of things hoped for, the evidence of things not seen". Notice that the scripture is not saying "things that do not exist". They do exist, but are not visible in the natural realm. It is the evidence of things not seen.

In the natural realm there are things that do exist that are not visible. We cannot see radio waves, but you know they exist when you place your food in the microwave oven and switch the oven on. By warming the food, the microwave oven has not made unseen radio waves visible. When we see the steam, it is not when those radio waves became real. They were already there. A microwave oven does not generate radio waves, but passes microwave radiation through the food, thereby causing the food to heat. But I am sure that you have experienced when you have tried to switch the microwave oven on and nothing happened. I am certain that the first thing you did was neither telephone the microwave manufacturer and complain that the microwave was no longer passing microwave radiation through your food, nor was it to telephone your energy provider and complain that they had removed you from the national grid; but rather it was to check and confirm that everything was working on your microwave oven. Specifically, you would have confirmed that the electricity was on, that the microwave oven was plugged into the wall socket, and that the distribution board in your house had not tripped. What I am implying is that you checked your microwave oven to see what was wrong with it. You trusted that the microwave manufacturer produced a reliable oven, and that your energy provider had not stopped providing electricity. You would not question that until you had eliminated all the possible problems with your microwave oven. Likewise, God is real and does exist. He just cannot be seen. We assume that because we have not experienced the victory in our lives that Jesus provided, nothing has happened. That is incorrect. We need to have more faith in God than we have in mankind and the natural realm.

The Bible has a very good illustration of this in 2 Kgs. 6. Elisha, the prophet of God, was revealing the Syrian's battle plans to the king of Israel. Every time the king of Syria tried to ambush the king of Israel, Elisha would warn the king of Israel, and he would counter the Syrian's ambush. This happened so often that the king of Syria finally concluded that there had to be a traitor present. He knew that the king of Israel could not be operating without inside information. When one of the servants to the king of Syria said that Elisha was revealing the words that the king of Syria spoke in his bed chamber to the king of Israel, the king of Syria sent his armies to capture Elisha. 2 Kgs. 6:15 records this event: "And when the servant of the man of God arose early and went out, there was an army, surrounding the city with horses and chariots. And his servant said to him, "Alas, my master! What shall we do?" (I have heard another minister say this was old English for 'he panicked'). Elisha knew why the Syrian army had come. Look at Elisha's comment to this situation in verse 16: "...(D)o not fear, for those who are with us are more than those who are with them".

People who do not believe anything exists beyond their five senses would say Elisha was lying. He was confessing that something was a certain way when in reality it was not, hoping that it would become so. But Elisha was speaking the truth. There were more with him than there was with the Syrian army. The fact is that Elisha's help was in the unseen realm. The key to understanding this illustration is to recognise that there is another realm of reality beyond this physical world. Those who are limited to only their five senses will always struggle with this. In the physical world you could count the Syrian soldiers by the thousands, and there was only Elisha and his servant. But in the spiritual realm, there were many more horses and chariots of fire around Elisha than there were Syrian soldiers. We read on in 2 Kgs. 6:17, and the scripture says, "(A)nd Elisha prayed, and said, 'Lord, I pray, open his eyes that he may see'. Then the Lord opened the eyes of the young man, and he saw. And behold, the mountain was full of horses and chariots of fire all around Elisha". Gehazi's physical eyes were already wide open. God was now opening his spiritual eyes. He was able to see with his heart into the spiritual world. And when the spiritual world was taken into consideration, then Elisha's statement was perfectly true.

Those who see faith as an attempt to make something real which is not real will always struggle with those who see faith as simply making what is spiritually true a physical truth. Those who limit truth to only the physical realm would have called Elisha a 'name it, claim it, blab it, grab it' cultist. But by saying that, they condemn themselves, and show they only consider what they can see, taste, hear, smell, and feel to be reality. They are what the Bible calls 'carnal' (Rom. 8:6-7). When Gehazi's spiritual eyes were opened, the Syrian army did not disappear. They were still there. The physical truth was still true, but there was a greater spiritual truth that emerged. True faith does not deny physical truth, but refuses to let physical truth dominate spiritual truth. True faith subdues physical truth to the reality of spiritual truth.

Because Elisha believed in the realities of the spiritual world, he raised his hand and striked the Syrian army with blindness. Then he led the whole Syrian army captive to the king of Israel! The Bible gives no indication that Elisha saw the horses and chariots of fire around him; but he did not need to see. He knew what was real in the spiritual world, and he controlled his emotions and actions accordingly. Those who operate in true faith do not need to see with their physical eyes. Their faith is evidence enough.

1.5 Operating in Faith

2 Pet. 1:2-4 affirms that all things that pertain to life and godliness are given to us through the knowledge of God. The 'all things' includes faith, because without faith it is impossible to please God (Heb. 11:6). Therefore faith must come through the knowledge of God. That is the reason Rom. 10:17 says that faith comes by hearing the Word of God. The degree of faith that you operate in is directly proportional to the revelation knowledge that you have of God through His Word. As a result, many believers have found it very difficult to operate in faith. This is because they either do not possess a real knowledge of God's Word in them, or they have allowed Satan to steal the Word from them. In the parable recorded in Luke 8:5-8 about the sower and the seed, Jesus portrayed several heart-types, and of these heart-types portrayed, Satan had no direct access to the seed expressed as the Word of God, because Satan cannot steal the Word from us if it is hidden in our hearts (Psa. 119:11).

Before God's Word can penetrate your heart, you have to understand (not comprehend) what it is saying. If the Word is not understood, then it will be like seed scattered on top of hard-packed ground (the wayside), where the devil can steal it away. Luke has linked belief and salvation (Luke 8:12) with the Word being sown in our hearts, in the same way as Rom. 10:14-17. If there is no Word, there cannot be any belief or salvation (1 Pet. 1:23). In addition, Luke's use of the word "saved" could include, but is not necessarily limited to, forgiveness of sins. Salvation includes much more than forgiveness of sins. Therefore, this verse could describe a believer who simply does not receive the Word in a certain area of his/her life and therefore does not experience the victory that Jesus provided for him/her. Subsequently, it is not really a faith problem that exists, but rather a Word problem. Once we truly believe in our hearts what God's Word says, we are well on the way to seeing what we believe materialise in the physical realm. For example, once we believe (have faith) that God has made provision for everyone to be healed (Psa. 103:3; Acts 10:38; 1 Pet. 2:24), we can begin to see people healed. If we do not believe that God heals everyone, our hearts become hardened to this truth, we will not see people healed, and we will develop what the Bible calls "an evil heart of unbelief" (Heb. 3:12). It was unbelief in God's Word that prohibited the Israelites from entering the promised land (Heb. 3:18-19), and unbelief will also prevent us benefiting from the "exceeding great and precious promises" (2 Pet. 1:2-4) which God has given us in the scriptures.

1.6 Abiding in the Word

You are not incapable of living a life of faith. Quite the contrary, as a born-again believer, you have already been given THE measure of faith as a part of the fruit of the Holy Spirit. Gal. 5:22-23 says "(B)ut the fruit of the Spirit is love, joy, peace, longsuffering, gentleness, goodness, **faith**, meekness, temperance: against such there is no law" (KJV, emphasis mine). Have you ever seen or heard a fruit tree struggling and complaining about how difficult it is to produce fruit? Of course not! It is natural for a fruit tree to produce fruit. It is even easier for a fruit tree to produce quality fruit when that fruit tree is protected from the elements of nature and given nourishment. So it is with a believer. Faith will automatically be the product of our abiding in the Word, which is Jesus (John 1:1; John 15:1-7). We as believers must avail ourselves of God's Word by placing it in our heart, so that the Holy Spirit may bring it forth at the appropriate time to accomplish a complete and total victory. We have all been given the measure of faith (Rom. 12:3), but continue to be defeated because of a lack of knowledge of how that faith works.

Mankind did not learn how to fly overnight. There were

many failures, but now no one doubts that the laws of aerody-namics work. Likewise, you will not learn all God's laws pertaining to faith overnight either; you may fail a few times before you start seeing faith produce that which it should. The law of faith, which created everything, is without a doubt more certain than the laws of aerodynamics. The knowledge of God and how faith works is hidden for you, not from you, in the Word of God.

If you are of the opinion that you require the knowledge of God, then pray this prayer as recorded in Eph. 1:15-21:

Heavenly Father, I ask that You give me the spirit of wisdom and revelation in the knowledge of You, that my understanding will be renewed; that I may know what it is that You require me to do for Your Kingdom, realise what You have provided me by grace through Jesus, and may abound and increase yet more and more through the knowledge of Your exceeding love toward me. I ask this according to the incredible greatness of Your power, being the same mighty power that raised Jesus Christ from the dead and seated Him in a place of honour at Your right hand in the heavenly realms, being far above all principality and power and might and dominion, and every name that is named, not only in this age but also in that which is to come. In Jesus' name, Amen.

Now, believe that you receive, and watch faith begin to be produced in your life.

1.7 The Measure of Faith

We have the same faith that Paul had. Paul said in Gal. 2:20, "I am crucified with Christ: nevertheless I live; yet not I, but Christ liveth in me: and the life which I now live in the flesh I live by the faith of the Son of God, who loved me, and gave himself for me". Firstly, I am quoting from the King James Version of the Bible as almost every modern English translation misinterpreted this verse from Greek and made it read, 'faith in Christ'. The commentaries have led us to believe that the phrase is really just an odd way of saying 'faith in Christ' and that it really refers to our faith in Christ. But such reckless handling of the Word of God, be it deliberate or otherwise, completely alters the meaning of the God-inspired scriptures. Paul did not say that he lived by faith IN the Son of God, but by the faith OF the Son of God.

The measure of faith that Paul had was the same measure that Jesus had. It was Jesus' faith. We could never be saved by our faith in Christ, were it not for the faith of Christ; and we can never be saved by the faith of Christ until we have faith in Christ. Yes, we must have faith in Christ; and our faith in Christ is the result of 'the faith of Christ' as our Saviour in this world. In addition, 'the faith of the Son of God' is referring to Jesus' faithful performance of all the Father wills as our covenant Surety, Substitute and Redeemer. Therefore, if there is only one measure of faith (Rom. 12:3), then we also have the faith of Jesus. Faith does not come and go as many believers think; it is constant. What does fluctuate, however, is (a) our perception of whether or not we have faith, and (b) how much faith we use or manifest.

We have the same quantity and quality of faith that Jesus has; therefore, we can do the same works that Jesus did, if we receive this truth and begin to use what we have (John 14:12). Because many believers have not understood this, they have spent their time asking for faith or for more faith. How is God going to answer a prayer like that? For example, if I gave you the keys to my car and then you turned around and asked me if you could use my car, what should I say to you? I would probably stand there surprised while I tried to figure out what you actually wanted, as I have given you the keys to my car and therefore, indirectly, given you permission to use my car. That is the reason there is not an answer from God when we plead with Him for faith, or more faith. We already have the same faith Jesus has. There is nothing more that God can give us!

Although we all have been given THE measure of faith, Jesus

did say that He had never seen such great faith as the centurion manifested (Matt. 8:10), and He also spoke of His disciple's little faith (Matt. 8:26). But He was speaking about how much faith He saw being used. None of us use all the faith we have been given. In that sense, some do have more faith than others, but technically, it is more faith that is being exhibited or that is functional. Most believers do not doubt that faith works. They just doubt that they have enough faith. The more you know about faith and how it works, the better it will work for you. If all you knew was that you have the same faith Jesus has, then that would remove hopelessness and motivate you. If Satan can blind you to this truth, then he can keep you from using the faith you have.

1.8 Using Faith to Access God's Grace

As I mentioned earlier, Peter explained that God, by His grace, has given us "all things" we need for life and godliness (2 Pet. 1:2-4). In verse 3, Peter tells us that access to these 'all things' is through the knowledge of Jesus. Paul also confirms that we gain access to God's grace through faith in Jesus (Rom. 5:2; 1 Cor. 1:4; Eph. 2:7-8). This is because Jesus is God's grace (being God's undeserved, unearned and unmerited favour). Grace is not a Bible subject, nor a doctrine, but rather a person, namely the Lord Jesus Christ (Rom. 5:17). When Jesus came, He brought in a new dispensation, and although the Old Testament Law did not pass away (Matt. 5:17-18), those who placed their faith in Jesus were no longer subject to the Law (Rom. 6:14; Gal. 3:24-25). There is only one gospel, and that is the Gospel of the Lord Jesus Christ; the Gospel of grace, which will bring you blessings, such as healing, prosperity, success, salvation, righteousness, protection, security, peace and wholeness, and this is only the beginning... it will bring you much, much more! If the blessings of God were subject to us keeping the Law, then we would warrant, deserve, and justify His favour. It would be our reward. But grace is underserved, unearned, and unmerited. Some ministers teach that to fall from grace means to become a castaway, or rejected. But this is incorrect, as it really means that you leave God's unmerited, unearned, undeserved favour and go back under the Law and start to work and help God to realise your blessings. As believers, we only have to believe God and His Word to experience His grace. Keeping the Law is 'deserved' favour; God's grace is 'undeserved' favour.

However, it is important to understand that grace by itself is not enough for us to receive salvation, deliverance and everything else that Jesus died to give us. God has made 'all things' available by grace, but we need to exercise our faith to partake of everything Jesus' sacrifice provided. If grace alone was sufficient, every person on this earth would be partaking of Jesus' sacrifice and experiencing salvation, peace of mind, healing, and total prosperity; because God's grace for salvation has appeared to all men (Tit. 2:11). Grace and faith need to work together, and neither is sufficient on their own. What God provides by grace can only be received by faith, and not by living a righteous life, fasting, praying, keeping the Law, or any other way we may think of. Grace certainly cannot be accessed by works or performance (Eph. 2:7-8); in fact, grace and works cannot be blended (Rom. 11:6). In Paul's Epistle to the Galatians, he warns that trying to earn grace by good works renders grace ineffective as far as we are concerned (Gal. 3:2-4), and says that it will result in us "falling from grace" (Gal. 5:4).

For this reason many believers are disappointed when, after having learnt and put into practice the mechanics of Christianity, being faith, confessing God's Word, giving and receiving, etc. and all the right-to-do things, the fruits of the Christian lifestyle neither materialise, nor do they receive what God has made available to them by faith. Faith is simply the hand that takes from the hand of God. We please God when we humble ourselves and take a position to receive from Him. By doing this we are allowing God to be Abba Father in our lives and He desires that. The Bible says that the lesser is always blessed by the greater (Heb. 7:7). But as it is with our nature, we are not good receivers. When you give someone a gift, you often hear them say, 'Oh no, you should not have done this', or 'I do not deserve that'. We all need to ask God to make us better receivers, and to enlarge our capacity to receive not based on how deserving we think we are, but based solely on His grace to supply and give. Choose to see His loving heart, His undeserved favour toward you, and generous supply, and reach out in faith and take from God.

Chapter 2

Your Authority In Christ

2.1 Introduction

God is the creator of all authority and power. When He created
mankind, He gave them dominion over the earth (Gen. 1:26-28).
God gave us authority and power to rule over this world,
without any restrictions thereon. Authority is a right conferred
by recognised social position. Authority often refers to power
vested in an individual by a superior, and in general is the
power, privilege, or influence over another of inferior rank or
position. God created angels to be ministering spirits to us (Heb.
1:14). Many believers will agree that Lucifer was a powerful,
beautiful angel created by God (Isa. 14:12), with pipes and
tambourines (musical instruments) built into his body (Ezek.
28:13). Lucifer was sent by God to the Garden of Eden to serve
and minister to Adam and Eve. He came to the Garden on a
divine mission; but once there, he transgressed.

The Bible reveals that angels, like us, also have a free will (2
Pet. 2:4). Although angels have a free will, there is no scriptural
evidence that their authority and power is unconditional like
ours. Therefore, if an angel transgresses against God, God will
simply revoke that angel's authority and power. Likewise, when
Lucifer rebelled against God, he lost his divinely delegated, God-
given power and became Satan. Satan is not using superior
authority and power against us, but rather he is using the same
authority and power that God gave mankind to rule and reign
over this earth. It is our own authority and power that he uses
against us.

2.2 God's Integrity

Lucifer came to the earth as an anointed angel on a divine

assignment from God to serve and minister to Adam and Eve. However, when he heard God give Adam and Eve unconditional authority and power on this earth (Gen. 1:26-28) without any restrictions or qualifications, he recognised an opportunity. Isaiah 14 reveals his consideration for this opportunity (Isa. 14:12-14). Lucifer envied God. He was not content with being 'the anointed Cherub who covers' on God's holy mountain (Ezek. 28:14). He was jealous and wanted God's position; but he could not just take that place with the delegated power he had been given. If he would have rebelled, that authority and power would have instantly been revoked by God. As a result, he saw an opportunity with man because God had given Adam and Eve something that He had never given to the angels, namely an unconditional, with no reservations or qualifications, authority over the earth (Psa. 82:6). Lucifer saw that if he could get Adam and Eve to yield this authority to him and rebel against God, then he could become the new 'god' of this world (2 Cor. 4:4).

Even thought the Bible had not been written at this time, Lucifer knew that the Word of God was settled from the beginning (Psa. 119:89), and that the Lord never changes (Mal. 3:6). Once God speaks, it is complete; and He never goes back on His Word. Psa. 89:34 states "(M)y covenant I will not break, nor alter the word that has gone out of My lips". According to Heb. 6:18 it is impossible for God to lie because "God is not a man, that He should lie, nor a son of man, that He should repent. Has He said, and will He not do? Or has He spoken, and will He not make it good?" (Num. 23:19). The integrity of God's word is what makes the universe exist and bind together. God upholds all things by the Word of His power (Heb. 1:3). God will not violate what He has said; so when He told Adam and Eve that they had dominion over all the earth, He meant it and could not cancel, revoke or go back on His Word. Obviously, the Lord never meant for mankind to turn that authority and power over to Satan, and because of God's integrity, once mankind did yield that dominion over to the devil, God could not stop and say "Oops, I did not mean for that to happen; let us start over again". That is what we would do if someone abused the privilege we gave them, but that is not how God operates. God is bound by His own Word and He has magnified His Word above His Name (Psa. 138:2).

2.3 Lucifer's Opportunity

Lucifer knew that he could not overpower God in a direct confrontation. Even if he did convince one-third of the angels to follow him and rebel against God, as is commonly cited in popular theology where it states in Rev. 12:3- 4 that the dragon took one-third of the stars and threw them to the earth, he still would never be able to dethrone God, who according to the same popular theology, retained two-thirds of the angels. Lucifer saw how God gave Adam and Eve an unconditional authority; and if they of their own free would yield to him, they would transfer that unconditional authority to him as well. As a result, he entered into a snake and used this serpent to speak to Eve and tempt her. Then he persuaded both Eve and Adam to eat of the forbidden fruit.

As Creator of the universe, God had the ability to destroy this world, including Adam and Eve, the devil, and all the angels that had rebelled, and start over if He so desired. Yet, to intervene in the affairs of this world would have violated His Word. He had given dominion over this earth to Adam and Eve, physical human beings. In principle, God could not prevent Adam and Eve from yielding their authority to Satan, and thereby making him the god of this world! Lucifer knew the love that God had for Adam and Eve and for that reason knew that God would not destroy His creation to whom He had provided with a free will. Satan did not pounce on and conquer Adam and Eve through force, but rather deception.

Many believers are of the opinion that Satan is an angelic being with supernatural power, able to oppress and suppress mankind; a common depiction of Satan in many films today. Satan and his demons are always depicted as these strong, powerful beings, able to cause pain and suffering as they please. But these believers forget that Lucifer lost his divinely delegated, God-given power the very instant he transgressed against God and became Satan. The devil is not using a superior power and authority against us. He is actually using the same authority and power that God gave mankind to rule and reign with over this earth. It is our own authority and power that he uses against us.

On his own, Satan is powerless. He depends completely on physical human beings yielding to and empowering him. Even under the Old Covenant, Satan did not have the power to control and dominate people. He has to use our own power to control and dominate people, and it is only as we submit to him by indulging his lust, lies, anger, bitterness, unforgiveness, fear, depression and the like that Satan is able to do anything. This is why our words and actions are so important...

2.4 Our Authority in Christ

As born-again believers, Jesus has restored that authority and power God gave to mankind, and much more. Adam and Eve were given authority over this earth, but after Christ Jesus rose from the dead, He had authority in heaven, authority on earth, and authority under the earth (Phil. 2:10). After Jesus' resurrection, and before His ascension, He said to His disciples "(A)ll authority has been given to Me in heaven and on earth. Go therefore and make disciples of all the nations, baptizing them in the name of the Father and of the Son and of the Holy Spirit, teaching them to observe all things that I have commanded you; and lo, I am with you always, even to the end of the age..." (Matt. 28:18-20). The authority we have as believers in Christ Jesus today is superior to the authority Adam and Eve had. Jesus has reclaimed all authority and power lost, as well as authority over the demonic realm (Matt.10:1, 7-8). By the way, 'Christ' (or

Khristós in the Greek) means 'anointed', and was used as a title for Jesus during His earthly ministry, therefore Jesus Christ / the Anointed. However, after Jesus' resurrection and ascension, and through His finished work on the Cross, this title became part of His name, and He therefore became known as Christ Jesus, or the Anointed Jesus (Acts 19:4; Rom. 3:24; 1 Cor. 1:2).

Compared to the Old Testament, there is a distinct difference in the way the New Testament refers to Satan. The Old Testament hardly mentions him, as there was no need for the Old Testament saints to have any knowledge of Satan as it would not have benefitted them to know that Satan was their adversary as they did not have the authority to rebuke and bind him (Phil. 2:10). The Old Testament saints were required to adhere to the Old Covenant (Mosaic Law), as this empowered God to move in their lives. The New Testament reveals that Satan is the source of sickness, disease, oppression, and the like; and unlike the Old Testament saints, we have an authority that has been given to us that enables us to confront and dispel Satan and his demons.

However, many believers are not using their God-given authority and power, and are allowing Satan to steal from them through sickness, disease, poverty, tragedy, or similar whilst confronting God and pleading with Him to intervene on their behalf. But God cannot intervene in your life if you are passive, as this negates His will and power in your life (Jas. 4:7). The Bible clearly mentions that we have "...power and authority over all demons..." (Luke 9:1). Many believers do not realise that Satan is dominating their lives. They think that the adversity they are suffering is due to circumstances or fate. The Bible says "(A)nd you He made alive, who were dead in trespasses and sins, in which you once walked according to the course of this world, according to the prince of the power of the air, the spirit who now works in the sons of disobedience, among whom also we all once conducted ourselves in the lusts of our flesh, fulfilling the desires of the flesh and of the mind, and were by nature children of wrath, just as the others" (Eph. 2:1-3). Before our spirits were born-again, we were by nature children of Satan. He exerted power and influence over our lives. 2 Cor. 4:4 further states "...whose minds the god of this age has blinded, who do not believe, lest the light of the gospel of the glory of Christ, who is the image of God, should shine on them". The devil is actively at work today hardening people and blinding them from the truths of the Gospel. This is not a passive battle; he is aggressively pursuing and trying to destroy people. One of the reasons why Satan has such a stronghold on so many people today is because the Church has not recognised the spiritual battle we are in.

2.5 Understanding Our Authority

Bear in mind that this authority and power that Jesus has restored to us only enforces God's spiritual law. We are not causing God to move, or perform on our behalf when we use the authority and power that Jesus has given us. In Isa. 45:11 we read "...concerning the work of My hands, you command Me". This verse undoubtedly explains that God has instructed us to direct the work of His hand, which is everything He has already provided through Christ Jesus, into manifestation. We are not the power source, but the power that Jesus has given us is under our control, under our authority.

Sickness, disease, poverty, tragedy, or similar will not leave an unbeliever that rebukes and resists, as they do not possess the power of God inside of them. This is what happened to the sons of Sveca (Acts 19:11-16). These men saw Paul expelling demons in the name of Jesus, and tried to do the same. But the demons inside the possessed man they were trying to set free rose up and caused the possessed man to beat these seven men, sending them fleeing. If you are not connected to the power source, being Jesus, you cannot exercise dominion over to the devil. Only once you are born-again and have received the power of the Holy Spirit according to Acts 1:8, then can you act on that God-inspired power, which is under your authority. However, merely praying for preservation, healing, wholeness and prosperity will not result in God dropping your inheritance on you as a believer from heaven. God's spiritual laws require us to step out in faith as our positive response to attain what He has already provided for us through His grace. God will not move in your life without your cooperation (see Chapter 3 regarding the sovereignty of God). You must be in agreement with Him and work in partnership with His spiritual laws. The release of God's power in your life is directly proportional to how you believe, and not proportional to your performance and good works. All of us come short, and the issue is faith. You get what you believe. If you believe that God has already healed you and you begin to exercise your authority, you will see that healing manifest. But if you believe that God can heal but He has not done it yet, then that healing will not transpire.

2.6 Obstructing Our God-given Authority

There are times when we just feel like speaking out our negative thoughts and emotions, as psychology today tells us that it is unhealthy to bury negative feelings. However, in light of the spiritual battle, we need to exercise our faith. In Matt. 6:31 Jesus states "...take no thought, saying..." (KJV). Therefore, a thought becomes your own when you speak it out of your mouth. You cannot keep thoughts from entering your mind. Kenneth E. Hagin used to say 'you cannot keep a bird from flying over your head, but you can keep it from landing there and building a nest'. Negative thoughts will come at times, but you have a choice. You do not have to entertain them. Negative thoughts and emotions do not have to become a part of you. If you do not voice them, they will not be yours.

The choices you make, the things you say, the actions you take, and what you believe about what is happening around you determines whether God or Satan dominates in your life. This spiritual battle is for your heart and the hearts of every other person on earth. God is trying to influence people and draw them toward righteousness and toward Himself, to live consistent with Him so that His blessings can manifest in their lives. Satan, on the other hand, is waging all-out war trying to steal the hearts of people away from God. He wants to fill their hearts with his condemnation and corruption. But Satan cannot control you outside of your will. He cannot do anything without your cooperation and consent.

Many believers choose not to believe that there is an intense spiritual battle happening right now, but whether they do or not, the fact is that it is taking place. Their unwillingness to engage in battle does not mean that the battle is not taking place; it just means that they are being influenced, controlled and used by the devil. Eph. 6:10-12 reads, "(F)inally, my brethren, be strong in the Lord and in the power of His might. Put on the whole armor of God, that you may be able to stand against the wiles of the devil. For we do not wrestle against flesh and blood, but against principalities, against powers, against the rulers of the darkness of this age, against spiritual hosts of wickedness in the heavenly places". This is referring to demonic powers. Notice that the verse says we are not wrestling against flesh and blood. Much that goes on in your life is not just human.

You need to constantly be aware that your words are either releasing life or death. Do not allow just anything to come out of your mouth. Set a watch before your mouth and speak only life (Psa. 141:3), because you will eat the fruit of your tongue. Prov. 18:20 says "(A) man's stomach shall be satisfied from the fruit of his mouth; from the produce of his lips he shall be filled". Every word you utter out of your mouth is a seed that produces after its kind. If you are moaning, complaining, and speaking out negativity, then that is the fruit you will reap in your life. You cannot keep a problem from happening, but you can keep the problem from dominating you by speaking out correct, positive,

God-inspired words. In this spiritual battle, Satan takes advantage of the words we speak. "For by your words you will be justified, and by your words you will be condemned" (Matt. 12:37). Believers do not realise just how important their words are. They speak foolishness, doubt, unbelief, and other things that allow Satan to devour them because they lowered their guard.

When we live in God's will and allow Him to bring His perfect plan for our lives to fulfilment, our lives are always much better than if we followed our own will. Obedience to God is good for us to pursue as it always produces peace, joy, and power in our lives, which are some of the fruits of the Spirit. Fruit comes as a result of abiding in the vine (John 15:4), and abiding in the vine involves being obedient (John 15:10). Obedience should begin in our thoughts, because those thoughts become our actions. Unforgiveness is birthed in how we think about people and situations. The more we dwell on the wrong that someone has done to us, the more angry and bitter we become. The Bible says "(F)or if you forgive men their trespasses, your heavenly Father will also forgive you" (Matt. 6:14); and in 1 Cor. 13:4-7 we read that "(L)ove suffers long and is kind; love does not envy; love does not parade itself, is not puffed up; does not behave rudely, does not seek its own, is not provoked, thinks no evil; does not rejoice in iniquity, but rejoices in the truth; bears all things, believes all things, hopes all things, endures all things".

The ability to love people is hindered when we stay angry and refuse to forgive. One of the snares Satan uses against believers to separate and divide, to weaken and destroy, and to obstruct fellowship with God is unforgiveness. Paul urges us to "(L)et all bitterness, wrath, anger, clamor, and evil speaking be put away from you, with all malice. And be kind to one another, tenderhearted, forgiving one another, even as God in Christ forgave you" (Eph. 4:31-32). At its root, unforgiveness is selfish, because it is all about how I feel and what has been done to me! When we are filled with unforgiveness we are filled with self. We are thinking about what has been done to us, and what someone did not do for us that they should have done. But what would happen if we thought more about what the person who hurt us is doing to him or herself by disobeying God and mistreating us? Thinking about others always pays great dividends and frees us from selfishness. You may have truly been treated unjustly, but turning inward and thinking only of yourself will not help you recover from your anguish. When God tells us to forgive our enemies and show them mercy, it seems to be the most unfair act in the world. Many believers feel that these instructions from God guarantee that others will take advantage of us. That would be true if there was no God. But when we follow these commands, be assured that the Lord is on your side. He said in Rom. 12:19, "(B)eloved, do not avenge yourselves, but rather give place to wrath; for it is written, 'Vengeance is Mine, I will repay'...". When we fight back, we are drawing on our own strength. But when we turn the other cheek, we are invoking God as our defence. Once we understand this, it becomes obvious that these instructions are for our own good. God knows the dangers of unforgiveness, bitterness and resentment and knows that to forgive is the only way for us to move past the anguish felt and into the good life that is waiting for us!

Letting God be the one who defends us is a matter of faith. If there was no God to bring men to account for their actions, then turning the other cheek would be the worst thing we could do. But we know that there is a loving God who takes the persecution of His children personally (Acts 9:4), and who promises that vengeance is His, and He will repay. Taking matters into our own hands shows a lack of faith in God and His integrity. Jas. 1:20 says that the wrath of man does not accomplish the righteousness of God. Regardless of how appropriate our anger may seem, and regardless of how we think our wrath could make a person or situation change, we will never achieve God's best that way. When we defend ourselves, we stop God from defending us. It has to be one way or the other. It cannot be both ways. When we turn the other cheek to our enemies, we are releasing the power of God on our behalf.

Judgment against those who persecute God's children will not always come in time to prevent their harm but as the scriptures make it very clear, God will avenge His own (Deut. 32:35; Rom. 12:19; Heb. 10:30). The Bible teaches us to put on love (Col. 3:14), which means that to extend love to others is something we prepare for and do purposefully. Even as Christ did not come to condemn the world and is not holding men's sins against them, even so, we have been given the same ministry of reconciliation. For those who do not receive the love we extend to them but rather take advantage of us because of our 'turning the other cheek', God will repay. 1 John 3: 10 reiterates this by saying, "(I)n this the children of God and the children of the devil are manifest: Whoever does not practice righteousness is not of God, nor is he who does not love his brother".

Chapter 3

God's Love For Us

3.1 Introduction

In the Bible we are told that God's very nature is love (1 John 4:16). God can never function contrary to His own nature. Never will you experience God conveying His will toward you other than as an expression of perfect love. God's kind of love (His nature) always seeks the very best for a person. He will never give you second best ... His nature will not allow Him.

God does however bring discipline on those who continue in sin and rebellion. But even His discipline is always based on love. "For whom the Lord loves He chastens, and scourges every son whom He receives" (Heb. 12:6). When a believer becomes anxious, wondering if God's will for their life is actually going to come to pass, that is when they do not really understand and know God and His immense love for them. 1 John 4:18 says "... perfect love casts out fear..." If we can understand the perfect love of God for us, it will banish all fear from our thinking.

3.2 The Nature of God

In the Old Testament we picture God as being angry, full of rage, judgement and eager to punish. Although this is how God will deal with those who do not accept the love and forgiveness of Jesus Christ, this is not the nature of God! But people who fashion their understanding of the nature of God based solely on the Old Testament do not get the correct representation of God. They use Old Testament scriptures as the basis for what they believe, not understanding that Jesus forever changed God's dealings with mankind. They do not understand the difference between the way God dealt with people under the Old Covenant and the way He now deals with us through Christ. Religious ideas, arising from a misunderstanding of scripture, hinder people from entering into a close relationship with God. Many people are afraid to come before God because they have been taught, or have been given the impression that God is going to "slap" them for whatever reason. As a result, they are of the opinion that they need to crawl and be fearful when coming before God. But that is not the relationship God desires, or that His Word teaches.

2 Cor. 5:19 says "...God was in Christ reconciling the world to Himself, not imputing their trespasses to them, and has committed to us the word of reconciliation". Under the New Covenant, God is not imputing our sins to us. That is the exact opposite of what happened under the Old Covenant. This is explained in detail in the New Covenant, and yet the Body of Christ has missed this truth. The vast majority of believers are still sin conscious, the very thing that Old Testament believers longed to be free from. They saw our covenant by faith and prophesied about the superiority of the New Covenant that God would make with mankind (1 Pet. 1:10-12). Yet, today's believers are not taking advantage of all the benefits of God's love available in this New Covenant. God's people are truly being destroyed for a lack of knowledge (Hos. 4:6).

In Luke 9:56 Jesus says "(F)or the Son of Man did not come to destroy men's lives but to save them". This was Jesus' response when His disciples James and John wanted to call fire down from heaven to consume the Samaritans. His rebuking to what His disciples wanted shows that God was dealing with people differently under the New Covenant as opposed to what we saw in the Old Covenant. Throughout the Gospels we read that Jesus went around healing all those who were oppressed by the devil. In other words, He was always doing good and benefitting mankind, and never caused any afflictions. Therefore, it is evident that oppression comes from Satan and not from God.

God has a perfect plan for every person's life (Jer. 29:11), but

He does not force us to follow His perfect plan. We are free moral agents with the ability to choose. He has told us what the right choices are (Deut. 30:19) but He does not make those choices for us. God has given us the power to control our own destiny. Jas. 4:7 says we are to "...submit to God. Resist the devil and he will flee from you". This verse makes it very apparent that some things are from God and some are from the devil. We need to submit to those things that are from God and resist those that are from the devil. The word "resist" means to "actively fight against".

John 10:10 states that "(T)he thief does not come except to steal, and to kill, and to destroy. I have come that they may have life, and that they may have it more abundantly". If a person really believed that God is the one who oppresses them because He is trying to work some good in their life, they should not resist this trying from God as this would be resisting God's plan. Obviously nobody promotes this for it is ridiculous. If hardship and problems make us better, then everyone who has had problems would be better for them, and those who had the most trouble would be the best. But this is contrary to what we see in everyday life. Believing that God wills everything to happen in your life, good or bad, gives us the ability to accept things that happen in the short-term but in the long-term this leads to passivity. By not actively resisting the devil will result in you becoming passive which will not cause Satan to flee from you as your passivity negates God's will and power in your life.

God does not directly control the events on earth, He has a good plan for us, but that plan has to have our cooperation in order to come to pass and we need to realise that any problems in our lives are from the devil, or from our own choices, or just as a result of living in a fallen world.

3.3 Sovereignty of God

The Church today leads us to believe that God controls us, and manipulates us independent of our will, and that nothing can happen without His approval. The Church has expanded the word "sovereign" to mean God controls everything, and that nothing can happen other than what He wills or allows. The dictionary does not define the word "sovereign" as meaning a deity controlling everything, nor does the Bible translate and use the word "sovereign" as meaning God controls everything. Rather, "sovereign" means having supreme rank, power, or authority.

In 2 Pet. 3:9, Peter said "(T)he Lord is...not willing that any should perish but that all should come to repentance". God has made us accountable for our own lives, and it is our free will that damns us, not God. This scripture undoubtedly highlights God's will for people concerning salvation, yet people are still experiencing despair. In Matt. 7:13 Jesus said, "(E)nter by the narrow gate; for wide is the gate and broad is the way that leads to destruction, and there are many who go in by it". God does not desire anyone to perish, but the Lord gave us the freedom to choose. He paid for the sins of the whole world (1 John 2:2; 1 Tim. 4:10), but we must choose to put our faith in Christ and receive His salvation.

God gave us dominion over the earth (Gen. 1:28), but mankind surrendered that dominion and power to Satan through his deceitful act in the Garden of Eden. As a result, Jesus was spoken into existence as the Son of Man to regain dominion and power on the earth, and restore mankind to their rightful position. Jesus made us co-heirs with Him, but God still cannot do anything on this earth without our cooperation. In Eph. 3:20 we can see this point made clear as it states "...according to the power that works in us".

If a person really believed that God is the one who places poverty, sickness, and adversity on them because He is trying to work some good in their life, why bother trying to alleviate this poverty by working and earning an income, or seeking medical assistance, or getting the elders of the church to pray over adversity, as these actions would be in direct disagreement with God's will and perfect plan for your life. These actions would then prohibit you from getting the full benefit of God's plan for your life. The belief that God controls everything independent of our free will is probably the biggest inroad we give Satan into our lives as we become passive in resisting him and do not exercise our faith. If God controls everything then our actions are irrelevant and our efforts meaningless; and I do not believe this is the abundant life promised to us in God's Word, nor for what Jesus was crucified.

Remember the story of how God asked Abraham to offer Isaac, his only son, in Gen. 22. I can imagine the heartache Abraham felt as he led Isaac, his promised son, up Mount Moriah to be sacrificed. But God provided a substitute, a ram, and Isaac did not have to be offered. That ram caught in the thicket was an illustration of Jesus, God's precious Son, who would one day be led up Mount Calvary to be crucified in our place for our sins. God so loved His Son, but He so loved you too, that He willingly gave up His Son for you to die on the cross. That is how much God loves you! And it is this truth that will help you to break down the barriers in life, conquer every pessimistic thought, and succeed in whatever you set your hands to!

Wrong thinking about the sovereignty of God is one of the biggest problems people have in experiencing God's love. If you believe God is the One who is causing all the problems in the world, it will definitely affect your relationship with Him. What if I told you I knew who has been orchestrating recent terrorist attacks, which has caused much affliction and destruction? Or I knew the reason why babies are born with birth defects and people suffer things like murder and rape. I am certain that you would pursue me and harass me until I told you who was orches-trating recent terrorist attacks, or the reason for human suffering in order to see justice being administered to those perpetrators! Yet, this is what the Lord is being blamed for every day. It is even written in our insurance contracts that major natural disasters and tragedies are "acts of God"...this is not a true representation of God. God is not the source of our problems. Understanding the sovereignty of God correctly is so important, and anyone who does not get a grasp of this will never truly appreciate God's love. It is impossible to feel good about God if you believe the accusers that depict Him as being evil.

The apostle Paul explains it like this in Eph. 3:14-17: "(F)or this reason I bow my knees to the Father of our Lord Jesus Christ, from whom the whole family in heaven and earth is named, that He would grant you, according to the riches of His glory, to be strengthened with might through His Spirit in the inner man...". This 'might' that Paul is talking about is actually power that comes as a result of having a revelation of something. The scripture continues by saying, "...that Christ may dwell in your hearts through faith; that you, being rooted and grounded in love...". Paul was praying for you to be rooted and grounded in God's love, so that you may be able to comprehend the love of Christ which passes all understanding, and be filled with ALL the fullness of God! This means that when you are rooted and grounded in God's love, you are truly strengthened with power, and have access to all that God is, namely: wisdom, strength, peace, favour, health, provision... There is no impossible challenge, no unattainable desire when you know that you are truly enabled by God's love.

3.4 God's Unconditional Love

Imagine the night before Jesus' crucifixion. He has communion with His disciples and washes their feet. He reveals that Judas is the one who will betray Him. He tells the disciples that He is leaving and they cannot come. Then, He speaks these words: "(A) new commandment I give to you, that you love one another; as I have loved you, that you also love one another. By this all will know that you are My disciples, if you have love for one another" (John 13:34-35). By virtue of the fact that this would be, in part, His final words to the disciples, they had to be very important. And notice that what He said to them was in the form of a command, not a suggestion.

I am sure that you have read or heard this passage many times before, but many believers do not think that this is something they can actually do. It is an aspiration that they strive to reach with gritted teeth, and usually with little success. It therefore begs the question of why would Jesus give His disciples a command He knew they could not keep?

The majority of churches today are teaching that God's love for us is conditional. However, through this teaching, they are misrepresenting His love, and it is one of the main reasons that we as believers are so judgmental and harsh toward other people. Consciously or not, we tend to treat people the way we believe God is treating us. We must understand that God does not love us because we are lovely. He does not love us because we read the Bible, go to church, pay tithes, or do our best to keep the command to love others as He loved us. The truth is that He loves us without conditions!

3.5 The Purpose for Our Existence

Many believers are made to think that they need to repay God for saving them by leading others to Jesus. It becomes such a part of their Christian philosophy that they start thinking that evangelism is the sole purpose for their existence. But then begs the question about Adam and Eve... they had no one to lead to the Lord, no Sunday school class to teach, no one to pray for, and no physical need of any kind. What was the reason for their existence? The answer and the reason can be found in Rev. 4:11 where it says "You are worthy, O Lord, to receive glory and honour and power; for You created all things, and by Your will they exist and were created". Therefore, it is evident that the original purpose of all creation was to give God pleasure. Adam and Eve were created for fellowship with God. He wanted someone to love and for them to voluntarily love Him back; and that is still God's purpose.

God's rationale for creating us was all about relationship. But we have come to believe that God loves us and acts on our behalf based on our performance. Therefore, we hold others to the same standard; our love for them is in direct proportion to their works, or how they treat us. Rom. 5:8 says "(B)ut God demonstrates His own love toward us, in that while we were still sinners, Christ died for us". God's love has never been, nor ever will be, conditional. He loved you at your worst, and most churches would agree with that. They concur that you are saved by grace through faith, no matter your past, but that is where grace stops and religion starts. Once you are saved, religion dictates that you should live holy, go to church, read your Bible, pay tithes, etc... If observance of these things were encouraged but not required, it would be good and pleasing to God. But religion always places the emphasis on the outward, or external. By making these actions mandatory in order to receive righteousness (justification), it perverts God's Word (Rom.14:1-6; Gal. 2:21). Thankfully, that is not how God sees us. In 1 Sam. 16:6-7 we read "(S)o it was, when they came, that he looked at Eliab and said, 'Surely the Lord's anointed is before Him!' But the Lord said to Samuel, 'Do not look at his appearance or at his physical stature, because I have refused him. For the Lord does not see as man sees; for man looks at the outward appearance, but the Lord looks at the heart". Samuel was going to choose Eliab to replace King Saul based on his outward appearance. But God was not looking at the outward appearance, but rather at his heart.

God is still concerned about your actions and behaviour. Under the New Covenant, it is not acceptable to lie, steal, commit adultery, or any other sin. However, He knows that those sins are the result of not having a relationship with Him. As long as you believe God is judging you according to your performance, you will never fully realise His love. Love is an action emanating from a decision, and God decided to love us even though we did not deserve His love. There is nothing you can do to earn His love; we need to just receive His love as a free gift.

3.6 Understand How Much God Loves You

When you understand how much God loves you, it becomes easy to love others. And when you love others as He has loved you, your behaviour will change towards them. If you loved your spouse or partner unconditionally, the way that Jesus loves you, you would never want to commit adultery. If you loved your neighbour as Christ loves you, you would never want to steal from them or give false testimony against them. How does the world know that we are disciples of Christ? John 13:35 says "(B)y this all will know that you are My disciples, if you have love for one another". This is exactly how the first-century Church evangelised the known world in thirty years. Not using televisions, the internet, email, or social media, but rather love for one another; which was so evident, it aroused eager devotion and enthusiasm.

A Pharisee once asked Jesus, "...which is the great commandment in the law". Jesus answered in Matt. 22:37-40, saying "'(Y)ou shall love the Lord your God with all your heart, with all your soul, and with all your mind'. This is the first and great commandment. And the second is like it: 'You shall love your neighbor as yourself'. On these two commandments hang all the Law and the Prophets". Like these Pharisees, many believers are still living with an Old Testament Law mentality. They are trying to earn the love of God who has already made the decision to love them unconditionally. Every believer has 'head' knowledge of God's love for them, but because of wrong thinking and religious teachings, it seldom translates into experience, as these things weaken that revelation of God's love.

Are you battling with sickness or depression? Are you faced with a financial lack? Are you handling a troubled relationship with your child, spouse or your boss? I encourage you to immerse yourself with a fresh revelation of God's love for you. This will cause you to have a renewed confidence of God's goodness toward you, and faith that God has already provided His fullness for whatever lack you are facing. In the midst of your challenges, instead of worrying and doubting if God is for you, you will have an energised and firm guarantee in your heart that if God did not withhold His one and only Son, He will not withhold anything good from you today! (Rom. 8:32) Surely, He is more than willing to bless your finances, grant you divine health, and give you favour with everyone you interact with. David said "I have been young, and now am old; Yet I have not seen the righteous forsaken, nor his descendants begging bread" (Psa. 37:25). Even when the devil starts throwing lemons at you, God will turn those lemons into refreshing lemonade for you! "Who shall separate us from the love of Christ? Shall tribulation, or distress, or persecution, or famine, or nakedness, or peril, or sword?" (Rom. 8:35). Tribulation, suffering or persecution cannot stop your heavenly Father's love from working on your behalf. His love for you is bigger and stronger than your financial woes, marital problems or health concerns. And when God's heart of love moves for His beloved, He opens doors that no one can shut and He makes a way when there seems to be none.

Therefore, more than anything else that you are pursuing, seek out the love of God for you. Live consciously of how deeply loved you are by God. Allow His perfect love to radiate on you in all its warmth and beauty. No matter what may be happening around you, you are safe and secure in His unconditional love. Let His love be an anchor for your faith, and expect good things to happen to you. We always win in the fight of life not because of our love for Him, but because of His love for us!

Chapter 4

Tithes and Giving

4.1 Introduction

The majority of churches I have been to teach rather emphatically that believers should tithe, that is, give ten percent of their income to their church. I have even heard some ministers say that if you do not tithe, God will not bless you. Like me, I am certain that when you hear a minister begin speaking on this subject, it is met with scepticism, with you wondering about the motives behind the message, as we all know of many Christians who tithe religiously but still experience lack and frustration in their finances.

There is more written in the Bible about finances than there is on heaven and hell, prayer, or faith. Jesus taught more about giving than any other subject, but never instructed ministers to take a tithe from believers. Therefore, it is important for us to distinguish between tithing and giving and see what the Word of God has to say about this subject.

4.2 The Old Covenant and Tithing

There are two schools of thought that profess that believers today are obligated to tithe ten percent of their income to the Church. One school of thought is of the opinion that we are still under the Old Covenant (Mosaic Law) and therefore are required to tithe, whilst the other school pronounce that tithing is part of the Abrahamic Covenant, being pre-Mosaic, and tithing is hence applicable to the believer as Abraham tithed by faith.

Considering the first school of thought, we need to understand what tithing meant to the Israelites after they left Egypt by bearing in mind Jas. 2:10 that states "(F)or whoever shall keep the whole law, and yet stumble in one point, he is guilty of all".

This is a New Testament warning of the consequences of trying to combine the Old Covenant that God made with the Israelites, of which there were 613 commandments, with the New Covenant that is mediated by Jesus. Many churches today have done just this and without knowing it, have become constrained to keeping the whole Mosaic Law, which the Bible says must be kept in full (not just one commandment).

God's purpose in giving the Law of Moses was to govern Israel until the Messiah came. Paul describes this Law in 2 Cor. 3:7 and 9 as a ministry of death and condemnation, and that is exactly what it was. The Israelites could only approach God through a system of sacrifices and a priesthood, and there were severe penalties for breaking the laws God commissioned. From the time of Moses until John the Baptist, this Law, as a two-sided agreement between Israel and God, governed the relationship between God and His people, where God would bless them if they kept their part of the agreement and He would curse them if they did not. It was an all or nothing arrangement. The Israelites could not choose which parts of the contract to adhere to, and which parts to ignore.

By mixing certain parts of the Old Covenant with the New Covenant, believers have "fallen from grace" because we are no longer in a contractual relationship with God through the Mosaic Law, but rather a relationship with God through a new covenant ratified by Jesus Christ, and not Moses.

The second school of thought states that tithing was not introduced under the Law, but it was regulated by the Law. As a result, tithing originated as an act of faith, and as faith transcends both the Old and New Covenant, by faith we should pay tithes as Abram paid tithes to Melchizedek, king of Salem, as an act of faith. This school of thought uses scripture from Genesis in a misguided attempt to prove that tithing was instituted prior to the Mosaic Law and is therefore relevant to the believer today. Their rationale is that because Abram gave ten percent of the spoils of war to Melchizedek (Gen. 14:20), and because Jacob chose ten percent as the amount to give to God for watching over him on his journey (Gen. 28:22), this is the prescribed amount God would have all people give.

The first mention of an offering (not a tithe) that is recorded in the Bible is in Gen. 4:3-7 where Cain brought forth an offering from the fruit of the ground to God and Abel brought the firstborn of his flock and of their fat. Without reading into these scriptures, there is no reference to a monetary tithe being made. We have two produce offerings being made.

Then, reading the fourteenth chapter of Genesis which deals with a battle between nine kings; Abram, with 318 of his men, went after the four kings who had conquered five cities, including Sodom and Gomorrah. These four kings had taken Lot, Abram's nephew, along with the people from the conquered cities, captive. Abram defeated the kings, and set his nephew Lot free. On his way back with all the spoils of war, goods of the enemy, and all the people from the conquered cities taken captive, the king of Sodom met Abram in the King's valley. Then, in Gen. 14:21, the Bible says that the king of Sodom said Abram could keep all the goods, he just wanted the people taken from the conquered cities returned to him. Abram responded in Gen. 14:22-23 by saying, "...I have raised my hand to the Lord, God Most High, the Possessor of heaven and earth, that I will take nothing, from a thread to a sandal strap, and that I will not take anything that is yours, lest you should say, 'I have made Abram rich'...".

It is apparent from this passage that Abram knew God was his source and was unwilling that there should even be an appearance that someone else was making him rich. Abram gave a tenth (or a tithe) of these spoils of war to Melchizedek. These "spoils of war" were not the original property of Abram, they were gained by defeating the four kings. In other words, Abram did not tithe on his personal possessions. Nowhere else, neither prior to nor after this event, is there reference made to suggest that the giving of a tithe on the spoils of war to Melchizedek may have been a tradition.

In Genesis chapter 28, Jacob the grandson of Abraham, spent the night at a place called Luz (almond tree). He had an incredible dream in which God reaffirmed the promise He made with Abraham. Jacob anointed the stone which was by his head where he slept and called the place Bethel, which means "house of God". Jacob then proceeded to make a deal with God, namely that if God would keep him safe on his journey, keep him clothed and fed, and bring him home safely, he would give God a tenth of what he received from God (Gen. 28:22). If Abraham had taught his children to tithe, then Jacob would not have tried to make a deal with God, but would rather have observed the good traditions instilled in him by his grandfather. The Bible, however, does not mention whether God accepted Jacob's vow, nor is there any mention that Jacob ever gave a tenth of all he received to God.

Although tithing is not a requirement for a New Testament believer, many do use tithing to discipline themselves as a way of giving. Although the legalistic giving of a tenth (tithe) does not please God, never the less, we are foolish if we do not freely and cheerfully give.

4.3 Blessings of Abraham

God's financial system is not like the world's system, and there are spiritual laws relating to giving. Giving is an act of worship and thanksgiving, as well as an act of faith; faith that God will endorse His spiritual law that the more we give, the more we will receive (Prov. 11:24-25; Luke 6:38). The Scriptures liken giving to sowing seed (Prov. 11:24; Gal. 6:7-8).

As I mentioned previously, Abram knew that God was his source and was unwilling that there should even be an appearance that someone else was making him rich. The Bible says "(N)ow may He who supplies seed to the sower, and bread for food, supply and multiply the seed you have sown and increase the fruits of your righteousness..." (2 Cor. 9:10). God is our source and we are simply a steward of the things He has entrusted to us, and giving will bring the kind of abundance God speaks of in His Word. In 2 Cor. 9:8 the Bible says "(A)nd God is able to make all grace abound toward you, that you, always having all sufficiency in all things, may have an abundance for every good work". The Word teaches that if we will be good stewards of all that God gives, ready to distribute to help meet the needs of others, God is able to make all grace abound toward us so that we have an abundance.

God wants us to give to promote His kingdom (Deut. 8:18), give to those in need (Eph. 4:28) and be blessed ourselves. But for this to happen, we need to be responsible in our giving and to understand the spiritual laws that apply. The first spiritual law involves our motivation for giving. The motivation behind your action of giving is more important than both the action of giving, and the gift itself. This is what is meant in the Bible where it says "(A)nd though I bestow all my goods to feed the poor, and though I give my body to be burned, but have not love, it profits me nothing" (1 Cor. 13:3). It is more blessed to give than to receive (Acts 20:35). By giving, you are neither giving up anything nor giving away anything; you are actually opening the door of blessing from God, which is another spiritual law. Like a farmer, when he sows seed, he does not see the act of sowing as throwing seed away. The farmer does this as an investment as he knows he will receive a harvest. Another spiritual law is giving with a cheerful heart (2 Cor. 9:7), which brings with it a sense of peace knowing that now the Master is responsible for you; your financial security does not depend upon you.

Many people believe that the money in their bank account, the motor vehicle in their garage, the family home, and anything else in their name – their financial security – belongs to them through the effort they have made to gain that financial wealth. But the Lord gives us His grace, which produces financial prosperity, so we can then abound to every good work. You may have laboured to earn that wealth, but it is God who gave you your life, your talents and abilities. You did nothing to achieve that. God is the one who gave you the ability to prosper. Deut. 8:18 says "(A)nd you shall remember the Lord your God, for it is He who gives you power to get wealth, that He may establish His covenant which He swore to your fathers, as it is this day".

To reiterate, the first step toward financial blessing is to recognise that God is your source. As long as you think it is your ability and your talent that causes you to prosper, you will probably have difficulty being faithful in that which is least. Jesus Himself said in Luke 16:10-11 that "(H)e who is faithful in what is least is faithful also in much; and he who is unjust in what is least is unjust also in much. Therefore if you have not been faithful in the unrighteous mammon, who will commit to your trust the true riches?" In other words, if you cannot deal with finances and become faithful in that, you cannot be trusted with anything. Finances are the foundation. If we desire to give more but are not able to because of a financial lack, then we are not really prosperous. True prosperity is not measured by the financial wealth we have accumulated, but rather by how much we are able to give.

Abraham is a great example of a man who had the mindset of a steward. He completely understood and acknowledged who his source was, and because of that, God abundantly blessed him. In Gen. 12:1-3 we read "(N)ow the Lord had said to Abram: 'Get out of your country, from your family and from your father's house, to a land that I will show you. I will make you a great nation; I will bless you and make your name great; and you shall be a blessing. I will bless those who bless you, and I will curse him who curses you; and in you all the families of the earth shall be blessed". There is much that can be said about this passage of scripture, but the important issue emerging from this is that this was not a kind of spiritual promise. As you read through the story of Abraham, you will realise that he was blessed, even when he did not act with integrity. For example, there was famine in the land of Canaan, and Abraham relocated to Egypt. Sarah, his wife, was very beautiful, and the Pharaoh desired her. But because of fear, Abraham lied about Sarah to the Pharaoh, and said she was his sister.

The Pharaoh included Sarah in his harem, but before any sexual relationship took place, God intervened through a dream and revealed the truth to the Pharaoh. Instead of the Pharaoh exacting punishment for this lie, the fear of God came upon him because he knew God was with Abraham. In fact, the fear of God was so strong in the Egyptians that they gave Abraham their servants, cattle, sheep, and more. From this you can see that Abraham received great wealth, not because of his astuteness, but because God had promised He would bless him, and the blessing was independent of what he deserved, independent of his performance. It was the favour of God in his life that caused him to prosper.

4.4 God is Your Source

God wants to prosper us so that we can bless others. That is what the Lord told Abraham, "I will bless you and make your name great; and you shall be a blessing" (Gen. 12:2). Paul said in Eph. 4:28 "(L)et him who stole steal no longer, but rather let him labour, working with his hands what is good, that he may have something to give him who has need". The reason we are told to labour is not to acquire wealth for our own needs, but to enable us to bless others! I know that this is a radical concept, but that is exactly what this verse is saying. Of course, Paul is not proposing that God will take responsibility for settling your debts and providing for your daily needs, but rather, he is speaking about priorities.

Again, like a farmer, there is always a waiting period between sowing and harvesting. Once the seed is sown, it needs to germinate and then grow, producing a plant that can eventually be harvested. When we give, there is a time between when we sow and when we receive, and during that time, we need to have some income in reserve to provide for our daily needs. Therefore, God expects you to use common sense when you give, and do not give everything you have and then find yourself in a financial squeeze. This is an important part of God's spiritual law, and by putting the Lord and His kingdom first, He will supernaturally take care of you.

Matt. 6:33 says "(B)ut seek first the kingdom of God and His righteousness, and all these things shall be added to you". The "things" that this verse is speaking of are what you eat, drink, and wear (Matt. 6:25-32). The Lord is saying that when we put Him first in our finances (and in our lives), He will see that our needs are met also. And when we give, it will be given back to us more abundantly than we gave (Luke 6:38). But again, if I can use the comparison of a farmer, no farmer will say that once they have sown seed that they regularly dig up that seed to inspect how its germination is progressing. They simply sow and wait for the harvest. In the same way, we should simply leave our gifts with God and not be concerned about the harvest, but remain in faith (Gal. 6:9) that He will bring forth a harvest at the right time (Mark 4:26-29). This is not to say that we can sit back, relax and expect God to drop bags of money from heaven. In 2 Thes. 3:10 the Bible clearly states that if you do not work, you do not eat. In other words, you are expected to labour, but you need to recognise that even though you labour, it is God's favour and blessing that brings the increase.

God gives seed to sowers (2 Cor. 9:10), or a more literal translation: God gives financial prosperity to Givers. I have heard it said that there are two types of people – those who are Eaters and those who are Sowers. With Eaters, it is all about them and what they can get for themselves. When they get seed, they eat it. But Sowers put others and, specifically, God's kingdom ahead of their own needs. When they get seed, they sow it. But God knows that Givers need to eat too. 2 Cor. 9:10 continues to affirm that the Lord will give you bread to eat and money to give. Actually, those who live to give will have more than those who live only to eat. The promise of this verse is declaring that if God can get money through you, He will get money to you. And here is a miraculous thing: as the money flows through you, there will always be more than enough to provide for your needs. The workings of God's financial system cannot be explained, you just have to put faith in this supernatural promise from God, as can be seen by the scripture "(T)here is one who scatters, yet increases more; and there is one who withholds more than is right, but it leads to poverty" (Prov. 11:24).

4.5 Promoting the Kingdom of God

You may hear that it is wrong for a believer to be financially wealthy. The Church will make reference to Jesus' account with the rich young ruler (Matt. 19:16-26; Mark 10:17-27; Luke 18:18-27). But when you read these scriptures in context you will notice that the young ruler's riches were not the problem, but rather the trust that this young ruler placed in his riches. And this is the danger that we as believers need to be aware of. Whilst prosperity can solve an immediate need, there is no substitute for placing your trust in Jesus. Jesus highlighted to His disciples that trusting in riches will almost certainly keep you out of the kingdom of God (Prov. 11:28; Mark 10:25).

But just because there are dangers associated with wealth does not mean we need to avoid being prosperous. There are dangers associated with electricity, but we do not avoid harnessing and utilising electricity to our advantage. The same mentality needs to be applied when working with wealth. Once we know the spiritual laws relating to God's financial system, we can harness these benefits and apply them for our benefit.

Deut. 8:18 tells us that it is God who gives us power to get wealth, and states the true purpose of having wealth from a biblical approach, being that wealth is to be used to promote the kingdom of God, and advance His plans for us. God himself is very rich (Psa. 24:1; Psa. 50:10; Psa. 89:11; Psa. 104:24). God enjoys riches, and we see this from the Biblical description of His tabernacle and temple (Exod. 25:1-9; Exod. 35:4-9, 21-28; 1 Chron. 29:2-9) and Biblical description of the future New Jerusalem (Rev. 22:18-21). In fact, God takes delight if we are financially prosperous (Psa. 35:27; 3 John 2). Although Jesus was rich, and He so much wanted us to be rich, He became poor so that through His poverty, we could become rich (2 Cor. 8:9). By putting God first in our lives, and not trusting in money, but rather in Jesus, God is more than willing for us to be financially prosperous so that we can promote His kingdom, and also enjoy His riches here on earth.

Chapter 5

Fasting

5.1 Introduction

Mention is made of fasting in the Epistles (New Testament letters to the Church), but the Church was neither instructed to fast, nor encouraged to do so. That is not to say that fasting should not be adopted by every believer, but your motive for wanting to fast must be attributable to a desire to want to spend time with God, and humble yourself before Him. Fasting can be used as a specific, yet practical means to humble yourself. David revealed through Psa. 35:13 that he used fasting as a way to humble his soul.

Lev. 16:29-31 states "This shall be a statute forever for you: In the seventh month, on the tenth day of the month, you shall afflict your souls, and do no work at all, whether a native of your own country or a stranger who dwells among you. For on that day the priest shall make atonement for you, to cleanse you, that you may be clean from all your sins before the Lord. It is a sabbath of solemn rest for you, and you shall afflict your souls. It is a statute forever", and introduces us to the ordinances for the Day of Atonement, which the Jewish people refer to as Yom Kippur. God provided a ceremony by which the High Priest went into the innermost sanctuary of the temple and made atonement. That was the appointment, the ordinance, for the Day of Atonement, the most sacred day on the Jewish calendar. We see in the New Testament (Acts 27:9) that the Day of Atonement was also referred to as 'the Fast'.

The essential nature of fasting is renouncing the natural to invoke the supernatural. The most natural thing for us to do is to eat. Yet, I have heard some ministers say that 'to fast' is neither simply nor necessarily to abstain from food, but from anything that hinders our communion with God. I have also heard 'fasting means to do without, to practice self-denial'. It is true that there are many things besides food that may hinder our communion with God. It is also true that we need to practice self-denial in general; but the fact remains that 'to fast' means primarily 'not to eat'; from the Greek word 'nesteuo', meaning 'to abstain as a religious exercise from food and drink' (KJV New Testament Greek Lexicon, Strong's Number: 3522).

5.2 Motive for Fasting

Nowhere in the New Testament did Jesus institute any kind of fast. In Matt. 6:16 Jesus said, "(M)oreover, when you fast, do not be like the hypocrites, with a sad countenance. For they disfigure their faces that they may appear to men to be fasting. Assuredly, I say to you, they have their reward. But you, when you fast, anoint your head and wash your face, so that you do not appear to men to be fasting, but to your Father who is in the secret place; and your Father who sees in secret will reward you openly". It was a Jewish custom to anoint one's self with olive oil and in Jesus' day it was apparently customary to anoint the heads of your guests as well (Luke 7:46). At times ointment or perfumes were used in this personal anointing. A lack of having one's head anointed was associated with mourning or sorrow.

Jesus is saying that there should be no external sign of fasting or sorrow, but it should be done secretly to the Lord to receive a full reward. Paul stated in 1 Cor. 7:5 that abstinence from the physical relationship in marriage for the purpose of fasting should not be done without the consent of one's spouse. In other words, a fast does not always have to be totally secretive to be productive. Rather, Jesus is dealing with the motives behind our actions. The fast must be directed toward God and not men. Fasting will not move God. He is the same before, during, and after you fast. But fasting will change you. It will help your mind discipline your body, and cause you to become more sensitive to the Holy Spirit.

5.3 Fasting in the New Testament

The Word of God mentions fasting again in Acts, but there is still no direction given to the Body of Christ on when to fast, or for how long to fast. In Acts 10 we read that Cornelius was fasting, even though he was not born-again at this stage. But being a Jewish proselyte, he naturally fasted according to his adopted tradition. In Acts 10:30 it says "...Four days ago I was fasting until this hour; and at the ninth hour I prayed in my house, and behold, a man stood before me in bright clothing..." The man being referred to was an angel, who instructed him to send for Peter in Joppa. But since Cornelius was a Jewish proselyte, and only saved once Peter came to his house, we cannot count this reference to fasting as being applicable to the Body of Christ.

Then in Acts 13:2 the scripture says "As they ministered to the Lord and fasted..." Here we read about five prophets and teachers that were ministering to the Lord, and fasting. The scripture stresses that they waited on God; but their fasting did not change God, rather it allowed them to become more sensitive to the Holy Spirit. The other references to fasting are in Acts 14:23 where the elders of the respective churches were ordained, and in Acts 27:9-35 where Paul was on route to Rome by sea and requested all on the ship to not go too long without food.

Therefore, as you can see from the above, there are no instructions given to the Body of Christ as to whether to fast or not. The records we have in Acts demonstrate that the people fasted as a means to minister to the Lord, ordain men to the ministry, or seek God in times of extreme danger. It seems the Lord would be pleased if we set aside some time to do likewise, provided you have a purpose. If you fast and do not minister to the Lord, it will not do you any good other than from a physical aspect only.

5.4 Paul's View on Fasting

Paul, in writing to the Church at Corinth, refers to the fact that he fasted, but neither encouraged them to fast, nor gave them any directions about fasting. In 2 Cor. 6:4-5 he confirmed that he indeed did fast by writing "(B)ut in all things we commend ourselves as ministers of God: in much patience, in tribulations, in needs, in distresses, in stripes, in imprisonments, in tumults, in labors, in sleeplessness, **in fastings**..." (emphasis mine).

Some might say that fasting is necessary to gain power to overcome the devil. Jesus, speaking about evil spirits, said in Matt. 17:21 that "...this kind does not go out except by prayer and fasting". But Jesus said this before He had died and was raised to newness of life, and soundly defeated the devil and all his cohorts. In Mark 16:17 Jesus says "...(I)n My name, they will cast out demons..." We do not have to fast to get the Name of Jesus. Fasting has nothing to do with casting out demons, but rather, it casts out unbelief.

5.5 Different Kinds of Fasts

In the Bible we are introduced to three different kinds of fasting which involved abstinence from food and/or drink.

For the sake of convenience, let us refer to the first and most common form of fast as *the normal fast*. What this comprises is simple from the fast Jesus followed after being baptised in the Jordan River. In Luke 4:2 we read "(A)nd in those days He ate nothing, and afterward, when they had ended, He was hungry". Jesus abstained from all forms of food intake, but He did drink. If Jesus had gone without food and water, I am certain that the scripture would have said that 'He was hungry <u>and thirsty</u>'. Therefore the normal fast is to refrain from eating only.

The second form of fast is *the absolute fast*. This fast comprises abstaining from both food and drink. Normally, this fast was never for longer than three days, probably because any longer periods may have proved physically detrimental. Our bodies can go for long periods without food and be physically benefitted, but only for a short time without water.

We read of Ezra that "he ate no bread and drank no water" (Ezra 10:6) as he was overcome with grief and astonishment of the shameful compromises of the people of Israel. When gravity threatened the Jewish nation with extermination, Queen Esther instructed Mordecai "...fast for me; neither eat nor drink for three days, night or day. My maids and I will fast likewise..." (Esth. 4:16). The Bible mentions that when Saul of Tarsus arrived in Damascus dazed and blinded by his encounter with the risen Christ, that "...he was three days without sight, and neither ate nor drank" (Acts 9:9). This spiritual revolution that was taking place within this Pharisee was not only to alter the whole course of his life, but to shape the history of the Church.

There is also evidence in the scriptures of absolute fasts that must have been supernatural in character due to their long durations. We read of Moses, that on two separate occasions went without eating and drinking for forty days and forty nights, whilst in the presence of God (Deut. 9:9, 18; Exod. 34:28). Then the journey of Elijah to Horeb appears to have been undertaken during an absolute fast, as we read in 1Kgs. 19:8 that after he "...ate and drank; and he went in the strength of that food forty days and forty nights as far as Horeb, the mountain of God". A journey of such duration through a barren desert, without further nourishment, constitutes a supernatural achievement!

The third and final form of fast is *the partial fast*. The emphasis here is on the restriction of diet rather than complete abstinence. In the book of Daniel we read about Daniel and his three companions, not wanting to defile themselves with the king of Babylon's rich food and wine, ask for vegetables to eat and water to drink. The steward set over them agreed to test the effect of this simple diet for a period of ten days (Dan. 1:8-15). Then again in Dan. 10:2-3 we read that Daniel "(I)n those days...ate no pleasant food, no meat or wine...till three whole weeks were fulfilled" while he sought understanding from the Lord pertaining to a vision he had received. 1Kgs. 17 introduces Elijah's spiritual preparation, and whilst at the home of the widow at Zarephath, he was sustained with simple cakes made from flour and oil.

5.6 What Can Be Accomplished

Fasting accomplishes many things, but the greatest benefit of fasting is that through denying the lust of the flesh, the heart, or the spirit, or the inward man gains ascendancy. Fasting was always used as a means of seeking God to the exclusion of all else. The real virtue of a fast is in humbling ourselves through self-denial. Endeavour to live a fasted lifestyle is an important part of our seeking God.

Chapter 6

Taking Communion

6.1 Introduction

Although the Church today understands the importance of doctrine, fellowship and prayer, very few believers understand the significance of Holy Communion, and this has caused much division amongst the Body of Christ. There are currently two extreme interpretations about the Holy Communion, and therefore misconceptions which have robbed many believers of an important God-ordained remembrance of the emotional and physical salvation that Jesus provided for us.

On one side of the spectrum, there are some who believe in transubstantiation, which teaches that the reality (the "substance") of the elements of bread and wine is wholly changed into the literal body and blood of Jesus Christ, while the appearances (the "species") remain unchanged. On the other side of the spectrum, there are believers who have reduced the Holy Communion to a mere ritual.

6.2 Understand the Elements

As a believer, you should partake of the Lord's Supper with full understanding of its significance. The Communion table is a symbol of Jesus' sacrifice for us. "And as they were eating, Jesus took bread, blessed and broke it, and gave it to the disciples and said, 'Take, eat; this is My body'. Then He took the cup, and gave thanks, and gave it to them, saying, 'Drink from it, all of you. For this is My blood of the new covenant, which is shed for many for the remission of sins'" (Matt. 26:26-28).

Not only should attention be given to the wine as a symbol of Jesus' blood that was shed for sin, the bread is a symbol of Jesus' body that was broken for us through His sufferings. He not only died for us on the cross but also bore 39 stripes on His back by which we are healed (Isa. 53:5; 1 Pet. 2:24). Partaking of communion should remind us of the emotional and physical salvation that Jesus provided for us.

The two elements of the Communion should neither be taken separately, nor treated as one. There are two elements because there is a two-fold application in the Communion.

The blood of Jesus is for the forgiveness of our sins. In Col. 1:14 we read "...in whom we have redemption through His blood, the forgiveness of sins". Similarly, in Eph. 1:7 Paul declares "(I)n Him we have redemption through His blood, the forgiveness of sins...". When you partake of the wine, place your trust in His blood, and know that you have been forgiven of your sins and have been made the righteousness of God (2 Cor. 5:21).

When we read of Jesus' interaction with the Syro-Phoenician woman regarding her daughter's healing (Mark 7:26-28), Jesus established that the bread, which is His body, is for our healing (the 'bread' mentioned in these scriptures refers to the healing that she was asking for, and the 'dogs' refers to non-Jewish or Gentiles, like herself). Having said that, I should clarify why the 'bread' refers to healing, and not deliverance. Acts 10:38 says that Jesus went about doing good and "...healing all who were oppressed by the devil..." From this we can see that disease and demon possession are both the results of oppression by the devil, and we need God's healing to overcome these. As we are now God's children, and New Covenant believers, we are fully entitled to partake of everything Jesus' sacrifice provided: salvation, peace of mind, healing, total prosperity, and much, much more!

6.3 From the Passover to the Cross

The Passover meal commemorated the Jews' deliverance from slavery in Egypt (Exod. 13:3-10). On the night of the original Passover, the Lord passed through the land of Egypt and judged the land by slaying all the firstborn men and beasts. The Jews had to slay a spotless lamb, take its blood and apply it to the door posts of their homes. They were commanded to remain indoors, under the covering of this blood until morning. When the Lord passed through the land at midnight to execute His judgment, He passed over the homes that had the lamb's blood on their doors and no one inside was harmed.

This is a perfect picture of the redemption that Jesus provides for us. The Lord was eager to share the Passover meal with His disciples (Luke 22:15). He was less than 24 hours away from fulfilling His mission and, like anyone who can see the finish line, He must have had feelings of relief and excitement. But this Passover meal would also have a much deeper spiritual application that, as Jesus explained in Luke 22:16, would be fulfilled through His death. Jesus was sacrificed on the fourteenth day of the first month of the Jewish year; the exact day and time that the Passover lambs were being slain. "For indeed Christ, our Passover, was sacrificed for us" (1 Cor. 5:7). Everyone deserves judgment because of their sins. However, Jesus provided Himself as a spotless, sacrificial lamb for us, so that if we apply His blood to our lives by confessing Him as Lord, God will pass over us on judgment day.

Most of us believe that in order to be saved, we need to ask God to forgive us of our sins, but that is not what the Bible teaches. In 1 John 2:2, it states that Jesus was the atoning sacrifice for our sins, and not only for ours, but also for the sins of the whole world. Jesus did not just die for those He knew would accept Him. He died for every sinner who has ever lived, and were still to live, on this earth. God is not waiting for us to ask Him to forgive us of our sins. The sins of the entire world – past, present, and future – have already been forgiven. John the Baptist said in John 1:29, "(B)ehold! The Lamb of God who takes away the sin of the world!"

In John 16:8-9, Jesus said, "(A)nd when He has come, He will convict the world of sin, and of righteousness, and of judgment: of sin, because they do not believe in Me". The Church often misinterprets this scripture and teaches that the Holy Spirit is here to convict you of all your sins. But this is not what the Holy Spirit is here to do. He is here to convict you of the single sin of not receiving Jesus as your Saviour. The only conviction is that of believing in Jesus Christ. People do not go to hell for committing adultery, stealing, or even murder. Those, like all sins, have already been paid for. This is what the Bible is saying in John 16:8-9; the only sin that is going to send a person to hell is the sin of rejecting Jesus Christ as his or her personal Saviour. The message that the Church is preaching today is causing us to become sin-conscious instead of Son-conscious (Rom. 3:19-22). It has also caused us to relate our performance to all the other blessings of God (refer to Chapter 1 regarding God's grace). Believers are being encouraged to repent from sin; however, in the New Testament we are actually encouraged to repent from dead works. Sin is the *fruit*, and dead works is the *root*. In Hebrews it states that the first foundation stone of our faith is repentance from dead works and of faith toward God (Heb. 6:1). Dead works are not the sins, but rather the so-called good works that people do in an attempt to gain righteousness with God. For example, if you partake in Holy Communion because you think that by doing this makes you right with God, that is a dead work. But, if you partake in Holy Communion because you know that you are right with God and understand the finished, complete and perfect work of Jesus at the cross, there will be power in that. From this you can see that although it is the same activity, the motivation for doing is completely different. One action is a dead work, while the other action is a living work by grace.

The word 'repent' in the Greek language is 'metanoeo', which means to 'change one's mind' (Thayer's New Testament Greek Lexicon: 3340). Religion has taught us that repentance is something that involves mourning and sorrow, and therefore we are influenced in thinking that there should be more preaching on repentance. However, Jesus said "(R)epent and believe in the gospel" (Mark 1:15). In other words He was saying to the Jews of His time: 'change your mind and believe the good news. For through My suffering and love for you, all your sins will be forgiven'. If you are still living under the Law and depending on your own efforts to qualify yourself and please God, it is time to change your mind from dead works and believe the Gospel.

6.4 Discerning the Lord's Body

Having established that the Holy Communion is a way for God to provide the believer with health, the next question is why are there so many believers experiencing sickness, and even premature death (Psa. 91:16)? I am not referring to suffering minor ailments and allergies, or even experiencing a cold; but rather severe, life-threatening illnesses. When a non-believer has an illness, it should come as no surprise as they lack the protection provided by Jesus. But when a believer is experiencing that same illness...

The Bible does provide the answer to this question. In 1 Cor. 11:29-30 Paul states that the one and only reason believers are weak and sick, and die prematurely is because "(F)or he who eats and drinks in an unworthy manner eats and drinks judgment to himself, not discerning the Lord's body..." The "unworthy" being referred to here is not about you being unworthy, as we are all unworthy of ourselves. Only Jesus makes us worthy through His blood when we are in Him. For that reason, this verse is talking about the manner, the way we take Communion. How often have you heard someone say, 'do not take Communion if there is any sin in your life, if you are living in sin, have unforgiveness in your heart, do not come to church regularly, do not belong to our church, etc.' I remember as a young believer I did not understand what was meant by "unworthy", and the consequences of "judgment"; but it was enough for me not to partake in the Holy Communion just in case I became another statistic. In church, every time the elements of the Communion were distributed, I passed them on to the person seated next to me. If you look at 1 Cor. 11:29 again, Paul is saying that if you eat and drink in an unworthy way, you bring damnation to yourself. But the word "unworthy" is an adverb, which gives more information about the verb, being in this case the eating and drinking. It is not describing the person who is eating and drinking. Therefore, Paul was not saying that if you are an unworthy person, do not partake. By not coming to the Lord's Table, I was robbing myself of God's source of health, healing and blessing. Next to salvation, health is the greatest blessing.

As we take Communion, we are solemnly proclaiming the Lord's death, and our union with Him through that death. This is a profession of our faith (2 Cor. 13:5) and therefore, there are serious consequences for those who profess something they do not possess. The Corinthians partook of the Holy Communion in an unworthy manner because they did not recognise that the broken body of the Lord was meant to bring them health and healing. Also, by treating the Holy Communion as a ritual, they missed out on God's blessings. They did not understand the significance of the bread. They did not know why they were partaking in the Communion. This is what it means to partake unworthily. The "judgement" that Paul refers to is not talking about being sentenced or convicted to hell, but rather a condemnation to weakness, sickness, and a premature death. It is also not the place of the Church, the Pastor, or the Elders to examine you and determine whether you are worthy to partake in the Holy Communion. According to 1 Cor. 11: 28 "...let a <u>man examine himself,</u> and so let him eat of the bread and drink of the cup" (emphasis mine).

6.5 The Power of Proclaiming the Lord's Death

A lesser known aspect of the Holy Communion is the power of proclaiming the Lord's death. Paul said, "(F)or as often as you eat this bread and drink this cup, you proclaim the Lord's death till He comes" (1 Cor. 11:26). This proclamation that Paul makes mention of refers to "Having disarmed principalities and powers, He made a public spectacle of them, triumphing over them in it" (Col. 2:15).

In other words, when we remember the Lord's death and partake in the Holy Communion, we are proclaiming to all demon spirits that they have been disarmed because He has triumphed over them, and He reigns. When you release your faith in the finished, complete and perfect work of Jesus at the cross, every knee must bow and every tongue confess that Jesus is Lord (Phil. 2:10-11).

6.6 How Often Can We Partake

The Lord's Supper comes from a part of the Passover meal that was celebrated only once a year. However, the early Christian Church took Communion weekly and sometimes daily. There is no specific frequency of the Lord's Supper prescribed in scripture. In fact, Jesus told us to have Communion often (1 Cor. 11:25), meaning there must be an important significance attached to this God-ordained remembrance.

As a believer, you as a royal priest (1 Pet. 2:9), are qualified to partake of the Lord's Supper, and even minister it to others. Do this as often as you need to, depending on your desire to receive health, healing, and blessings, from that one perfect sacrifice that abounds at His Table!

6.7 Partaking of the Holy Communion

Let us now partake of the Lord's Supper and release faith for our forgiveness and healing. But before you partake, just know that God wants you to "...prosper in all things and be in health, just as your soul prospers" (3 John 1:2). Prepare the bread (which ideally should be unleaven bread as leaven in the Bible represents sin, and Jesus is the perfect, sinless Son of God) and wine. Get ready to personally experience afresh His love for you...

Hear Him say to you, "take, eat, this is My body, which is broken for you". See His eyes ablaze with love as He says to you, "this cup is the new covenant in My blood, which is shed for you". See the Lord carrying all your sins and disease. He took your sins in His body on the cross. See Him taking in His body your physical conditions too. Whatever illnesses you might have, see it in His body. It is no longer in you. See His health and healing come into you.... Surely He bore your sins and carried your diseases. As you partake, release your faith in the bread and wine.

Take the bread in your hand, break it because His body was broken for you, and say this:

Thank you Jesus for Your broken body. It is for my healing, my spouse's healing, my children's healing and our family's healing. Thank you that by Your stripes, by the beatings You bore, by the lashes that fell on Your back, we are completely healed. I believe and I receive.

(Eat the bread)

Next, take the cup in your hand and say this:

Thank you Jesus for the new covenant engraved in Your blood. Your blood has brought me forgiveness and washed me from every sin. I thank You that Your blood has made me righteous. And as I drink, I celebrate and partake of the inheritance of the righteous, which is preservation, healing, wholeness and prosperity.

(Drink the wine)

Thank you Jesus, I love you because you first loved me!

Chapter 7

Speaking In Tongues

7.1 Introduction

You will notice that seven gifts of the Spirit (1 Cor. 12:7-11) were manifest in Jesus' earthly ministry, but tongues and the interpretation of tongues were not. You also will not find speaking in other tongues and the interpretation of tongues demonstrated in the Old Testament (although this gift was prophesied in Isa. 28:11). These two gifts are distinctive of the Holy Spirit, and became evident on the Day of Pentecost as recorded in Acts 2, and therefore occurred after Jesus' earthly ministry.

Jesus mentioned this new gift that God would offer believers under the New Covenant. In Mark 16:17-18, Jesus declared that five supernatural signs are to follow those who believe, one of them being that "...they will speak with new tongues..." Yet, there are many believers that do not speak with other tongues. We can assume several reasons for this, and probably a major reason is pertinent to the individual. But the key reason why there are still many believers that do not speak with other tongues is because there have been very little scriptural teachings on the value of speaking with other tongues.

7.2 Receive All the Holy Spirit Offers

Many believers are confused about the word 'baptism'. They think there is only one baptism available to the believer, and for that reason mistake the baptism *with* the Holy Spirit (Acts 1:5) with being baptised *by* the Holy Spirit into the Body of Christ (1 Cor. 12:13). Consequently, Eph 4:4-5 is misunderstood as there being only one baptism. When Paul said "(T)here is one body and one Spirit, just as you were called in one hope of your calling; one Lord, one faith, **one baptism**..." (emphasis mine), taken in context of this passage, Paul was referring to the one baptism that saves a person, being the baptism into Christ through the new-birth. This is the same baptism into Christ mentioned in 1 Cor. 12:13, where it states "(F)or by one Spirit we were all baptised into one body..." However, in Heb. 6:1-2, the Bible mentions baptisms; being plural, referring to all the baptisms available under the New Covenant.

Jesus also referred to two distinct experiences between the work of the Holy Spirit in the new-birth and the infilling of the Holy Spirit. In John 14:17, Jesus was referring to the new-birth experience when He said "...but you know Him, for He dwells with you and will be **in you**" (emphasis mine). Whereas in Acts 1:5 and 8, Jesus was conveying a different experience with the Holy Spirit when He said "...for John truly baptised with water, but you shall be baptised with the Holy Spirit not many days from now... But you shall receive power when the Holy Spirit has come **upon you**..." (emphasis mine).

Many churches today teach that there is no experience beyond the new-birth; you have all the Holy Spirit there is to have once you are born again. But this is only partly true. The Holy Spirit is present in the new-birth, to bear witness with your spirit that you are a child of God (Rom. 8:14, 16). The Bible describes the new-birth experience as "...received Him..." (John 1:12), "...given us eternal life..." (1 John 5:11), and "...receive forgiveness of sins..." (Acts 26:18). However, when we read the Book of Acts, it mentions that *they received* the Holy Spirit, were *filled with* the Holy Spirit, were *baptised with* the Holy Spirit, and *received the gift* of the Holy Spirit. All four these experiences were the same, but were all experienced after a person was born-again.

As a final word on this, if we take a look at Acts 8, we can see that salvation and the baptism in the Holy Spirit are two separate experiences:

Acts 8:12-17

12 But when they believed Philip as he preached the things concerning the kingdom of God and the name of Jesus Christ, both men and women were baptised.

13 Then Simon himself also believed; and when he was baptised he continued with Philip, and was amazed, seeing the miracles and signs which were done.

14 Now when the apostles who were at Jerusalem heard that Samaria had received the Word of God, they sent Peter and John to them,

15 who, when they had come down, prayed for them that they might receive the Holy Spirit.

16 For as yet He had fallen upon none of them. They had only been baptised in the name of the Lord Jesus.

17 Then they laid hands on them, and they received the Holy Spirit.

From the above we can deduce that Philip went to the city of Samaria and preached Christ unto the people. The people believed his preaching concerning the kingdom of God and the name of Jesus and were baptised, both men and women. According to Mark 16:16, Jesus said "...He who believes and is baptised will be saved..." The Samaritans believed in Jesus and were baptised. Therefore, they were saved, born again, before Peter and John arrived to lay hands on them. Also, verse 14 states that the Samaritans had received the Word of God, meaning they had received Jesus (John 1:1, 12, 14). And according to 1 Pet. 1:23, the Samaritans were born again, not of corruptible seed but incorruptible, through the Word of God which lives and abides forever. Hence, according to Jesus and the apostle Peter, the Samaritans were saved before Peter and John were sent to the city of Samaria. When they arrived, they did not pray for the salvation of the Samaritans, but rather for the infilling of the Holy Spirit!

7.3 The Infilling of the Holy Spirit

Reading the Book of Acts, it is evident that speaking with other tongues is always manifested when someone is baptised with the Holy Spirit, and is the initial supernatural evidence that that person has received the infilling of the Holy Spirit. In fact, there are five recorded instances in the Book of Acts where someone was baptised with the Holy Spirit.

In Acts 2:1-4 we read that on the Day of Pentecost that the disciples gathered in the upper room where "...they were all filled with the Holy Spirit and began to speak with other tongues..." Then in Acts 8:5-17, although there is no distinct mention that the Samaritans began to speak with other tongues after they received the Holy Spirit, Simon the sorcerer saw some outward manifestation that the Samaritans had received the Holy Spirit (Acts 8:18). What Simon saw could not have been miracles, casting out of demons, or healings, as this he had already seen take place in verses 6-7; nor could it have been great joy as he saw this in verse 8. Remember, he possessed esoteric knowledge, or expertise that harboured magical powers, so whatever he saw had to be something extraordinary. What Simon saw was something that produced evidence that could be seen with the physical eye, and be heard by those standing nearby, being the same supernatural manifestation that happened in Acts 2 when the 120 disciples were all filled with the Holy Spirit and began to speak with other tongues. Acts 2:33 says that Peter stood up and said "...having received from the Father the promise of the Holy Spirit, He poured out this which you now <u>see</u> and <u>hear</u>" (emphasis mine). The people gathered together in Jerusalem on the Day of Pentecost saw and heard the 120 Spirit-filled believers speaking with other tongues. And evidently, Simon saw and heard the same thing.

Next we read in Acts 9:10-18 where Ananias is instructed by Jesus in a vision to go lay hands on Saul of Tarsus that his sight may be restored and be filled with the Holy Spirit. Remember,

Saul was converted on the road to Damascus when Jesus appeared to him in a blinding light (Acts 9:1-9). I say this because in verse 6, Saul asks Jesus "Lord, what do You want me to do?" thereby confessing Jesus as his Lord, and he certainly believed that God had raised Jesus from the dead as he was talking to the resurrected Jesus (Rom. 10:9). Also, when Ananias met Saul in verse 17, he addressed Saul as 'brother'; not a salutation you go around saying to unregenerate murderers! Once more, this passage does not say anything about Paul speaking with other tongues. Yet, later we read where Paul said "I thank my God I speak with tongues more than you all" (1 Cor. 14:18). Again, the only logical deduction we can make is that Paul started speaking in tongues when he was filled with the Holy Spirit.

Ten years after the Day of Pentecost, an angel of God appeared to Cornelius, a devout Roman centurion, and instructed him to send men to Joppa and enquire at the house of Simon the tanner for a man named Peter. When Cornelius' three household servants arrived at Simon's house, the Holy Spirit instructed Peter to go with them. The following day Peter left with them for Cornelius' house, accompanied by some brethren from Joppa. When they arrived, Peter preached the Gospel to Cornelius and his entire household (Acts 10:1-43). In Acts 10:44 we read "...the Holy Spirit fell upon all those who heard the word" and verse 46 states "...they heard them speak with tongues and magnify God".

The last recorded instance can be found in Acts 19. Approximately 20 years after the Day of Pentecost, Paul had travelling to the city of Ephesus, and met with believers who had not heard about the Holy Spirit. Ephesus is located in Asia Minor, and as a result the Ephesians were not aware of what had happened in Israel. In Acts 19:6 Luke records that as Paul "...laid hands on them, the Holy Spirit came upon them, and they spoke with tongues and prophesied".

The above recorded instances prove conclusively that

believers who desire to be filled with the Holy Spirit will speak with other tongues. In addition, when you read through these five instances of people being filled with the Holy Spirit again, you will notice that after the initial outpouring, people never again waited, or tarried, to be baptised in the Holy Spirit. In Luke 24:49 Jesus instructed the disciples to "...tarry in the city of Jerusalem until you are endued with power from on high". They had to tarry because the Holy Spirit had not yet been poured out on the earth to carry on Jesus' ministry. On the Day of Pentecost, Jesus' words in John 16:13 ("...when He, the Spirit of truth, has come...") were fulfilled, and the Holy Spirit came like a rushing mighty wind to this earth, and He has been here ever since. From that day on, it has not been about us waiting on Him to come, but rather us receiving Him.

7.4 Receiving the Holy Spirit

In 1 Cor. 14:14 Paul says "(F)or if I pray in a tongue, my spirit prays, but my mind is unfruitful". What Paul was saying was that when we pray in our spirit, our mind and understanding plays no part therein. This is because the Holy Spirit gives us the utterance, or the ability, and helps our born-again spirit to pray to God (Acts 2:4; Eph. 6:19); but He does not perform the physical act of talking, which is done by the believer. This is the supernatural element of speaking in tongues. It is not who is speaking, but where the tongues are coming from, and what is being said. Acts 2:4 explains this by stating that "...they were all filled with the Holy Spirit and began to speak with other tongues, as the Spirit gave them utterance".

After a believer asks Jesus to be baptised with the Holy Spirit, (s)he needs to quieten their mind in order to sense the Holy Spirit's prompting from the inside to utter one or more vowel sounds with one or more consonant sounds. If nothing is sensed, the problem may be that you are not yielding yourself to the Holy Spirit. As the Bible says "(F)or with stammering lips and another tongue He will speak to this people" (Isa. 28:11). You need to wait in the presence of God through prayer, and as you do that, you will begin to discern the voice of the Holy Spirit. He will speak to your born-again spirit and let you know how to stay in God's perfect will in every area of your life.

7.5 The Value of Other Tongues

As you study Paul's Epistles, you will notice that he wrote much on the subject of tongues, and valued speaking in other tongues. This is evident from his statements "I thank my God I speak with tongues..." (1 Cor. 14:18), and "I wish you all spoke with tongues..." (1 Cor. 14:5). You would not thank God for something you did not value, or something of little importance; nor would you desire other believers to follow something you were opposed to. Many believers know that other tongues are the initial evidence of the baptism of the Holy Spirit, but are ignorant about the value of speaking with other tongues.

I have heard some ministers quote 1 Cor. 12:7-11 and say that Paul placed little significance on speaking in other tongues as it was at the end of the list of gifts manifested by the Holy Spirit. Also, 1 Cor. 14:19 is routinely interpreted that Paul took a sombre view regarding tongues and discouraged the Corinthians from speaking in tongues. To address these misconceptions, the gifts of different kinds of tongues, and the interpretation of tongues from the Holy Spirit is at the end of the list for no reason. This misconception is caused by someone complicating the content within a verse and adding their own interpretation to the verse. Similarly, if we look at 1 Cor. 13:13 it says "(A)nd now abide faith, hope, love, these three; but the greatest of these is love". Love is mentioned last, but is the most important. We need to accept that the Bible is the actual Word of God, and to be taken literally, word for word. Looking at 1 Cor. 14:19 again, and specifically the context of the passage, Paul was stating that the purpose of other tongues is not for teaching or preaching, but rather for a believer's own personal spiritual edification. In other words, during a church service, everything should be done to edify or build-up those in attendance. If all those in attendance are praising God together in church, it is perfectly acceptable to praise God in other tongues simultaneously. But nobody will be edified or built-up if they are speaking over the minister in other tongues, or the minister speaks in other tongues without any interpretation to those in attendance.

To continue, the value of speaking in other tongues is to communicate with God supernaturally. The Bible says "(F)or he who speaks in a tongue does not speak to men but to God, for no one understands him; however, in the spirit he speaks mysteries" (1 Cor. 14:2). In addition to this divine means of communication, Satan cannot comprehend what you are saying when you are praying mysteries to the Father, and that is a main reason for him causing much ignorance in this area, as he cannot get in on the conversation! And I say 'divine means of communication' because if you look at 1 Cor. 14:2 again, it says "...does not speak to men but to God..." (emphasis mine). Once we are filled with the Holy Spirit, we now have a means to communicate directly with God, spirit-to-Spirit, thereby excluding our mind and emotions from the conversation (1 Cor. 14:14).

In John 4 we read about Jesus stopping outside of Sychar to rest, and sending His disciples into town for food. Jesus notices a Samaritan woman coming to draw water at the well, and initiates a conversation. In verse 20, the Samaritan woman says to Jesus "(O)ur fathers worshiped on this mountain, and you Jews say that in Jerusalem is the place where one ought to worship". Jesus answers her and says "God is Spirit, and those who worship Him must worship in spirit and truth" (John 4:24). When you pray in other tongues, your spirit is in direct contact with God, being a Spirit. With that said, there will be occasions when we need to articulate our prayer, being either to petition God, repent for sin, ask for things, or intercede, in our known language. For this reason, we need to pray with the spirit, and with the under-standing (1 Cor. 14:15).

Another value of speaking in other tongues is for spiritual edification. In 1 Cor. 14:4 Paul says "(H)e who speaks in a tongue edifies himself...". Similarly, Jude 20:20 says "But you, beloved, building yourselves up on your most holy faith, praying in the Holy Spirit". By praying in other tongues, we revitalise our born-again spirit by the power of the Holy Spirit. Furthermore, to speak in other tongues is to pray according to God's perfect will. The Holy Spirit not only knows God's perfect will, He will always guide us in keeping with the Word of God. Paul mentions this in Rom. 8:26-27 when he says "...the Spirit also helps in our weaknesses. As believers, we know how to pray, but we do not know what to pray, or in other words, we do not know what the content of our prayer should be. But the Spirit Himself makes intercession for us...He makes intercession for the saints according to the will of God".

There are many reasons why we are not able to pray as we ought to, as we can only comprehend the situation from a natural perspective. But the Holy Spirit can assist us to pray appropriate to the perfect will of God. When a situation arises that you do not have knowledge about, we can say to the Holy Spirit, "Holy Spirit, I do not know what to pray for as I ought regarding this situation, but You do, so please help me pray". Then start to speak in other tongues, and He will be faithful in giving us the utterance, and help your born-again spirit to pray to God.

Chapter 8

Prayer

8.1 Introduction

Prayer is communion with God. It is fellowship, a connection, and a time for intimacy with Him. It should not be an activity, a ritual, or an obligation. Prayer is conversation with God, meaning it is both listening and talking. Prayer is your time to simply visit with God. However, most believers see prayer as an opportunity to "move" God. They believe that He can do anything, but that He has not done everything. And if this is your understanding of prayer, this may be the reason why you are not seeing results from your prayer life.

When the disciples asked Jesus how to pray (Luke 11:1), He had to deal with the misconceptions concerning prayer before He could teach them the proper way to pray (Matt. 6:5-8). The religious system had become, as it is today, hypocritical and false and Jesus had to undo what they commonly thought prayer was before He could effectively teach them what pray is meant to be.

8.2 Moving God

The book of Ephesians is written from the perspective that everything is already ours in Christ. Eph. 1:3 says, "(B)lessed be the God and Father of our Lord Jesus Christ, who has blessed us with every spiritual blessing in the heavenly places in Christ...". Any blessing we could ever need or desire from the Lord is not something to strive for but something we already have. God made the provision before we had the need.

The motive for our prayers should not be to "move" God. God has done His part by giving His Son, Jesus. His grace has provided everything through the sacrifice of Jesus. There is absolutely nothing we can do to earn God's grace, and there is nothing we can do to lose it either. If He has already provided for your needs by His grace, then prayer should merely be our positive response through faith to what He has already done, and not something we do to get God to respond to us. When Jesus cried "It is finished" (John 19:30), He meant just that. His work on earth was done. The atonement was complete. He provided everything we could ever need. We are not waiting on God to give, but rather God is waiting on us to receive.

8.3 Other Misconception about God

We need to understand that God is no longer attributing our sins against us. In 2 Cor. 5:19 the Bible says "...God was in Christ reconciling the world to Himself, not imputing their trespasses to them, and has committed to us the word of reconciliation". We are reconciled to God through Jesus, meaning we are in harmony with God. That is what the angels proclaimed at the birth of Jesus in Luke 2:14 which says, "(G)lory to God in the highest, and on earth peace, goodwill toward men!" The angels were not declaring peace on earth and an end to all hostilities and battles between people on earth. This is evident when looking back at world history. The angels were proclaiming an end to the war between God and man. God's wrath and justice has been satisfied through Jesus. He loves the world, and not just the Church. The Scriptures say in 1 John 2:2, "(A)nd He Himself is the propitiation for our sins, and not for ours only but also for the whole world". Jesus paid a price that was infinitely greater than the sins of all men. As a result, God's mercy extends to all people.

In the Old Testament, God's judgment was poured out on both individuals and nations. Man had not yet been reconciled to God through Jesus. Both individuals and nations needed a mediator, someone to intercede with God on their behalf, and that is where we encounter the likes of Abraham and Moses pleading with God. In Gen. 18:23-25, we read about Abraham interceding with God on behalf of Sodom and Gomorrah; "(A)nd Abraham came near and said, 'Would You also destroy the righteous with the wicked? Suppose there were fifty righteous within the city; would You also destroy the place and not spare it for the fifty righteous that were in it? Far be it from You to do such a thing as this, to slay the righteous with the wicked, so that the righteous should be as the wicked; far be it from You! Shall not the Judge of all the earth do right?'" In fact, Abraham negotiated with God until He agreed not to destroy Sodom and Gomorrah for the sake of ten righteous people. But there were not even ten righteous people in Sodom and the neighbouring city of Gomorrah. Similarly, in Exod. 32:12, Moses was pleading with God for the nation of Israel, and told the Lord "... (T)urn from Your fierce wrath, and relent from this harm to Your people". It was appropriate for Abraham and Moses to act as a mediator because Jesus had not yet come, and the atonement for man's sins had not yet been made. God and man were not reconciled.

However, as New Testament believers, this is not the way we should approach God. In the New Testament, God's judgment was poured out onto Jesus, and because of Him, man has been reconciled to God. We are no longer getting what we deserve; we have what Jesus paid the price for, if we will only believe. Jesus is now the Mediator (1 Tim. 2:5). Jesus has made all that God is and has, available to us, and it is through faith that we access that grace (Rom. 5:2). As Jesus is now our Mediator, it is wrong to continue to pray the way Moses and Abraham did. Under the New Covenant, Jesus is the only mediator needed to stand between God the Father and mankind. Sin is no longer a problem with God (not that I am advocating sin; see Chapter 6). Our sins have been atoned for, and we are now the righteousness of God in Christ Jesus. That is how God sees us, and when we under-stand that, it will change the way we pray.

8.4 Our Authority through Prayer

We have the authority to change the world through prayer. When God said: "(A)nd let them have dominion…over all the earth…" (Gen. 1:26), He was ensuring that the partnership with mankind was effective for the accomplishment of His purpose. God influences things to come to pass on earth when we are in agreement with His perfect will; and prayer is significant for effecting God's will. That said, God has given us an earthly license for heavenly interference. Prayer is not an option for the believer, but a necessity. If we do not pray, God cannot interfere in earth's affairs. It is imperative that we take responsibility for the earth and determine what happens here through our prayers. In Matt. 16:19 we read Jesus explaining to His disciples "(A)nd I will give you the keys of the kingdom of heaven, and whatever you bind on earth will be bound in heaven, and whatever you loose on earth will be loosed in heaven". Also, in 2 Chron. 7:14 we read God's answer to Solomon's prayer; "(I)f My people who are called by My name will humble themselves, and pray and seek My face, and turn from their wicked ways, then I will hear from heaven, and will forgive their sin and **heal their land** " (emphasis mine).

These scriptures are evidence that we have the authority and prerogative to determine what happens on earth. Furthermore, when we look through the Bible at God's interactions with both individuals and nations, we can see that every action taken by God was done with the involvement of a person:

- to rescue humanity in the flood, He needed Noah;
- for the creation of a nation, He needed Abraham;
- to lead the nation of Israel, He needed Moses;
- to bring back Israel from captivity, He needed Daniel;
- to defeat Jericho, He needed Joshua;
- for the preservation of the Hebrews, He needed Esther; and

- for the salvation of mankind, He needed to become a man.

God works through people to accomplish His purpose. If we have a financial need, God cannot, and will not, counterfeit money and make it appear in your hand; nor will He drop a money bag from heaven. If you need to sell your house, God is not personally going to buy your house. God supplies your requested provisions through people. If the Lord did not need our cooperation to see His power manifest, there would be no sickness on earth today. Nobody would suffer ailments and allergies, or even experience a cold. The Church would be experiencing revival, and the destruction happening on the earth would cease.

8.5 Is God Hearing You

Unanswered prayers are a major obstacle that hinders a believer's life of true faith. All of us have experienced when we did not believe that our prayer was answered. However, in Matt. 7:7 the Bible says, "(A)sk, and it will be given to you; seek, and you will find; knock, and it will be opened to you". As many believers can cite experiences where they asked for something and did not receive, the easiest explanation given is that we have misinterpreted Matt. 7:7 and it does not mean what it appears to say.

Then we read in Rom. 3:4 where it states "...let God be true but every man a liar..." This is one of the causes for a doctrinal division amongst the Body of Christ. The Word is sound in its doctrine, but when someone tries the Word and does not see the promised results, rather than admit that they could have failed, they say something like, "that must have passed away with the apostles" or "it must not have been God's will", etc. God is not the one who failed to answer, but rather we are the ones who have failed to receive.

What actually happens when we ask in prayer is that God moves immediately and gives us the answer in our spirits. We are responsible for believing that, and acting accordingly by faith to bring the answer into the physical world. God is a Spirit (John 4:24), and He always answers back to our born-again spirit. Through faith, we then give physical substance (Heb. 11:1) to what God has done. In other words, we convert God's answers to our prayer into a physical reality through our actions. That is not to say that it is us who produces the answer by our own power, but rather it is God who works the miracle, and it is manifest through us. Eph. 3:20 says, "(N)ow to Him who is able to do exceedingly abundantly above all that we ask or think, **according to the power that works in us**" (emphasis mine).

Daniel prayed two prayers in Dan. 9 and 10. He saw an answer to his first prayer while he was still praying, which was within about three minutes. But in the tenth chapter, it was three weeks before he saw his prayer answered. Some people would think, "why did God answer the first prayer in three minutes and the second prayer in three weeks?" The answer to that question is that God did not answer one prayer in three minutes and the other one in three weeks; He answered both prayers instantly. In Dan. 9:23, the angel Gabriel told Daniel that at the beginning of his prayer, the Lord gave him a commandment to go explain the answer to Daniel, and it took Gabriel approximately three minutes to get there. Then in the tenth chapter, the messenger who came to Daniel told him that on the first day of Daniel's prayer, the Lord sent him, but he had been hindered by a demonic power for three weeks. God was not the variable in these instances! He answered both prayers instantly, but what the Lord had commanded in the spiritual realm was hindered from manifesting in the physical realm.

Now you can understand better what Mark 11:24 means when it says, "...whatever things you ask when you pray, believe that you receive them, and you will have them". You receive in your spirit by faith whatever things you ask immediately, and it manifests in the physical later. It may be one minute, one day, or one year; but you cannot waiver in your belief that God has already answered your prayer. The time that it takes for God's answer to be manifest in the physical is dependent upon many things, but it is not God who determines that. God answers immediately. Remember, the scripture says that you must believe that you receive "when you pray". God is not asking you to believe something that is not true. You do receive instantly in your born-again spirit, but there is time before it is manifest in the physical.

Whether it be Satan, people's wills, unbelief, or any of a number of other possible hindrances, it is important that you know that it is not God who is unpredictable (Psa. 102:27; Mal. 3:6). In fact, this is a fundamental truth that you must be established in before you can even begin to do anything about speeding up the answer to your prayer. If you have prayed a prayer in line with God's Word, God answers it immediately (1 John 5:14-15; Dan. 9, 10). If you understand that, then you are ready to begin releasing your faith over bringing that answer into complete manifestation.

8.6 We Are Deceived

Satan is behind much of the wrong teaching on prayer. Consider how crafty his plan is and the fruit it produces. He has convinced believers to remain in their prayer closets, and take the place of Jesus as mediator through intercession. They spend hours in prayer pleading with God to turn from His wrath, to pour out His Spirit on the earth, and to meet the needs of the people. And whilst these believers are deceived in thinking that they are doing a good work, their family members, colleagues and peers are going astray, never experiencing the fullness of what God has planned for them. The Bible does not say that salvation comes through intercession, but by the foolishness of preaching (1 Cor. 1:21). And we are not told to pray for the sick, but to heal the sick (Matt. 10:8) by commanding healing into their broken bodies.

We have been deceived into believing prayer is all about persuading God to release His power. We believe He can save, heal, and deliver but that He is waiting on us to earn it. The truth is, we do not deserve His unmerited favour, and we will never be good enough to deserve it. God, by grace, has already provided everything we will ever need, and it is not dependent of any worth or value from us. Because of Jesus, all that God has is ours. We no longer need to beg or plead; but rather, we need to exercise the authority He has given us and receive His blessings.

There are, of course, scriptures in the Bible that proclaim that asking is a valid use of prayer, but our prayer life should not only consist of petitioning God, repenting for sin, asking for things, or intercession. Adam and Eve did not approach God in that way. They had nobody to intercede for, no demons to cast out, and no spiritual kingdoms to destroy. They had no need for clothes, food, accommodation, suitable employment, and therefore made no such petitions; yet they met with God in the cool of the day and communicated with Him. I do not believe that their conversations with God involved lack of, need for, sin and repentance, begging, or pleading. They prayed, had communion, and fellowshipped with God every day!

8.7 Physicality of Prayer

Prayer becomes a religious act when we use it in a way that God did not intend. This is the reason why many believers today are experiencing a lack of direction, little to no victory over Satan, poor spiritual progress, a weak witness, poverty and other similar problems. Praying for long periods of time, or at a specific time in the day, using certain words, phrases, mannerisms, or dramatic vocalisation will not impact your communion with God.

As God is with us always (Heb. 13:5), we should always be in prayer. Prayer is communicating with God. Prayer is conversation with God, meaning it is both listening and talking. This does not need to be performed through specific body positions. In the Bible, people knelt, raised their hands, and even looked up at the heavens. But you should not make a religious form out of these positions as an act of "prayer". You can pray with your eyes either open or closed; with your hands raised into the air, or hanging beside your body; standing, kneeling, or face down. Since meditation is prayer (Psa. 5:1) you do not have to pray out loud either.

We all have daily responsibilities and routines that consume the majority of our day. Even with our hectic schedules though, we make time for our spouse or partner. Similarly, we need to make time to commune with God in the midst of our daily responsibilities and routines. Just as it is unrealistic for us to limit our relationship with our spouse or partner, and only express our love and admiration to them at specific times, so too is a partial relationship with Jesus naive. God wants us to have a mature relationship with Him where we just enjoy each other's companionship.

8.8 The Model Prayer

"In this manner, therefore, pray..." Matt. 6:9. Jesus did not intend for us to recite "The Lord's Prayer". Jesus was giving us a model for prayer, not something to repeat, as what He taught against in Matt. 6:7.

Matt 6:9 "...(O)ur Father in heaven, Hallowed be Your name..." is a spiritual principal that Jesus was stating. We are to begin our prayers by entering into His presence with praise and worship (Psa. 100:4). As you enter His presence, remember that He is your heavenly Father. He is not upset with you. God is not condemning you; He is pleased with you and loves you dearly. Every New Testament believer has a close, personal relationship with God that supersedes even the very best of what Old Testament saints had. Therefore, begin every prayer by acknowledging your special relationship with God, and enter His gates with thanksgiving and praise. Thank Him that He is holy and kind, pure and good. Praise Him for being your Father and not your judge.

In Matt 6:10 "...(Y)our kingdom come. Your will be done on earth as it is in heaven..." Jesus continued to praise God and assert that it is the Father's will for things to be done on earth, as they are done in heaven. In heaven there is neither sickness, poverty, nor lack. Therefore, it is not God's will for you to have sickness, poverty, or lack in this life. We need to take this part of the model prayer as a guideline and pray that what is already waiting for us in heaven will manifest itself here on earth. This will allow God's will to be done here on earth as it is in heaven!

Notice that Matt 6:11 "...(G)ive us this day our daily bread..." is not a question; nor is it an arrogant demand. It is similar to a child asking of their parent for something to eat. It shows familiarity, which is the result of the parent's love for that child, and thereby gives that child the confidence and boldness to make such a demand. This is exactly how God wants us to interact with Him. He desires that we are familiar with Him through His love for us, and approach Him boldly (Heb. 4:16). There is no reason for us to approach our heavenly Father begging and pleading, and persuading Him to move for us. God has already done everything for us, and has provided everything that we need. We need to reach out in faith and take it.

Matt 6:12 "...(A)nd forgive us our debts, as we forgive our debtors. And do not lead us into temptation..." is not a prayer for a New Covenant believer. When Jesus cried "It is finished" (John 19:30), He meant just that. His work on earth was done. The atonement was complete. Jesus became sin for us (2 Cor. 5:21), through no wrongdoing on His part. He took our sin in His own body on the cross (1 Pet. 2:24) so that we might be made the righteousness of God in Him (2 Cor. 5:21). The spirit that we had which was dead unto God, is gone, and the new spirit which we received at salvation, is righteous, holy, and perfect (Eph. 4:24).

Once you have believed and received the Lord, your sins – past, present, and future – are forgiven.

God will never lead you into temptation. If an earthly parent would not do that to their child, how could we ever think that God, who loved us first (Eph. 1:4-5, 1 John 4:9) would do that to us. Jesus made mention to these things before the cross and resurrection. He was led into temptation on our behalf and overcame the devil (Matt. 4:1-11). If you are being led into temptation, you can be assured that it is not God (Jas. 1:13-14).

As Matt. 6:13 states "...(B)ut deliver us from the evil one..." our soul and body have been purchased by Jesus' blood, and our born-again spirits have been eternally redeemed (Heb. 9:12) from the prince of this world (John 12:31). Through faith in Christ, we have been delivered from the kingdom of this world (Rev. 1:6). Satan lost his legal hold over us, and we are now part of God's kingdom (1 John 5:4-5).

As Christ's model prayer began with praise, it is concluded with praise: "...(F)or Yours is the kingdom and the power and the glory forever. Amen" (Matt. 6:14). This is how we are to pray; we should begin with praise and end with praise. Phil. 4:6-7 tells us, "(B)e anxious for nothing, but in everything by prayer and supplication, with thanksgiving, let your requests be made known to God; and the peace of God, which surpasses all understanding, will guard your hearts and minds through Christ Jesus". When you pray with thanksgiving, the peace of God will keep your heart and mind.

Praise will build you up spiritually and keep you from destruction, "...for the joy of the Lord is your strength" (Neh. 8:10). Paul and Silas praised God in prison. It was their praise that released the power of God and the earthquake that delivered them from their captivity.

Chapter 9

Knowing God's Word

9.1 Introduction

Never has it been more apparent than now that the Church needs an anchor. In this past century alone, an estimated 200 million Christians were murdered for their faith, more than any other century in human history. The day is coming when God's Word, the fixed anchor, will be our exclusive source. The Body of Christ needs to come to an even deeper understanding that God's Word will endure any amount of pressure that the secular world places upon it, because it is higher than the heavens and it has been established by God Himself.

9.2 God Spoke into Existence

One of the most amazing truths in the Bible is that God spoke into existence everything that we can see and beyond into the vast reaches of outer space. It is totally incredible that God made everything, from the grass we walk on to the stars in the night sky, by simply speaking them into being...

It is therefore evident that nothing can stand in the way of God's words. There is no force in the universe that can refute, come against, or deny the power in God's overwhelming and unassailable Word. The Bible is God's Word, and none of His Word is void of power or impossible of fulfilment. Psa. 33:6 and 9 says "(B)y the word of the Lord the heavens were made... For He spoke, and it was done". The Bible says that God's voice literally shook the mountain of Sinai when He spoke (Exod. 19:18). Paul also referred to this occurrence in Heb. 12:26 where it states "...whose voice then shook the earth..."

God's Word cannot be opposed. It overcomes and conquers all that it is sent forth to defeat. Neither is there a circumstance that God's Word cannot prevail over; nor is there a problem in your life that God's Word cannot surmount. The Scripture declares that even the very pillars of heaven tremble at the words that God speaks (Job 26:11). Therefore, we need to learn to speak God's Word, as all our needs and desires can be supplied and satisfied through the Word of God. Psa. 12:6 declares that "(T)he words of the Lord are pure words, like silver tried in a furnace of earth, purified seven times". Likewise, in 2 Cor. 1:20 we are assured that "...all the promises of God in Him are Yes, and in Him Amen, to the glory of God through us". Finally, God promises us in Phil. 4:19 that He "...shall supply all your need according to His riches in glory by Christ Jesus".

9.3 What Are You Saying

Many believers do not realise that the words they speak have power, and we often speak them as though they are meaningless. Because of that, most believers at one time or another have been hung by their tongue. In Matt. 12:36-37 it says "(B)ut I say to you that for every idle word men may speak, they will give account of it on the day of judgment. For by your words you will be justified, and by your words you will be condemned". These words that we speak have a direct effect upon the hearers of those words.

For example, the words spoken to a child as (s)he leaves for school in the morning will impact on that child's success or failure during the day. If you are constantly telling a child that they are a failure and that they will never succeed in anything they do, those words will stay with them and bear fruit in their life. Similarly, kind words spoken to your partner or spouse in the morning can contribute to a sense of well-being as those words edify and build-up the hearer of those words. Words either encourage and edify, or contaminate and diminish the hearer's self-belief.

I am certain that you have experienced a pressurised situation at one time in your life, and someone spoke reassuring, encouraging and optimistic words to you. Suddenly there was an easing of the pressure, and you felt calmed and composed. But, I am certain that you have also experienced being calm and composed when someone suddenly spoke insensitive and incensed words to you, and you felt provoked and irritated. The words we speak are very important, and they determine what fruit will be produced in the lives of those whom the words are spoken to. Therefore, if our words are that powerful, can you imagine how much more powerful and electrifying are the words of God! Therefore, it is important for us to be filled with God's life-giving Word (John 6:63), and to hide His Word in our hearts.

Heb. 4:12 says "(F)or the word of God is living and powerful, and sharper than any two-edged sword, piercing even to the division of soul and spirit, and of joints and marrow, and is a discerner of the thoughts and intents of the heart". God's Word is so powerful that it can divide our soul from our spirit. Separating our soul or spirit from our body is an obvious distinction to make, but to tell our spirit from our soul is not simple. Even separating marrow and bone is an arduous task as the two are closely related elements of the body that work together almost inseparably. Yet the Word of God can not only separate joints or bones from marrow, but it can also separate the soul of man from the spirit of man.

9.4 Living and Powerful Word of God

The Body of Christ has not realised the authority and capability within God's Word. The knowledge of God's Word has not been abiding in us, or the carnal knowledge of the world has choked the Word of God that was there. The Bible warns us that we cannot serve two masters (Matt. 6:24) and that a double-minded man is unstable in all his ways, and cannot receive anything from the Lord (Jas. 1:7-8). If believers knew these truths, they would spend more time in meditating and studying God's Word, and giving it first place in their heart.

Matt. 6:22 gives us the promise that if the eye is single, we will be full of light. That means that if all your attention is focused on God through His Word, then the only thing that you will be full of is God and what His Word produces. This is a spiritual law that is repeated in Rom. 8:6, which says "(F)or to be carnally minded is death, but to be spiritually minded is life and peace". If you are experiencing anything but life and peace, it is because we are carnally minded. You cannot have life and peace without the knowledge of God.

The carnal knowledge that we dwell upon in our thought-lives is Satan's in-road to us. One of the main reasons I believe that the people we read about in the Pentateuch (the first five books of the Bible) lived to be as old as 969 years is because they did not know how to die; they did not even know that there was supposed to be a flu season every year. It took many years for Satan to pervert the knowledge that was in man so that (s)he would accept defeat. Most of our battles could be avoided if we would just be wise concerning that which is good and simple concerning that which is evil (Rom. 16:19).

9.5 Battle of the Mind

Our actions are a direct result of our thoughts. Rom. 8:5 states "(F)or those who live according to the flesh set their minds on the things of the flesh, but those who live according to the Spirit, the things of the Spirit". In other words, only those who walk after the Spirit are seeing the righteousness of the Law fulfilled in their lives (Rom. 8:4). This is because whatever a person thinks about is what (s)he is going to become or do (Prov. 23:7).

Many of the problems being experienced today by believers are rooted in their thinking patterns. Satan offers wrong thinking to everyone, but as believers we do not have to accept his offer. The devil is a liar. Jesus referred to him as "...the devil...there is no truth in him...he is a liar and the father of it" (John 8:44). He lies to everyone through nagging thoughts, suspicions, doubts, fears, speculations, and interpretations. But Jesus tells us in John 8:31-32 how we are to overcome the lies of Satan. We must get the knowledge of God's truth in us, and use this knowledge to compare what is in our mind with what is in the mind of God; and any thought that attempts to exalt itself above the Word of God we are to cast down and bring into captivity to Jesus Christ (2 Cor. 10:4-5).

The 'weapons' mentioned in 2 Cor. 10:4-5 is the Word of God received through teachings, books, Bible study and the like. We must abide in the Word until it becomes revelation, given by inspiration of the Holy Spirit. In Mark 4:24 Jesus says "...with the same measure you use, it will be measured to you..." We must continue using the *weapon* of God's Word.

The Bible provides many detailed instructions on what we are to think about, namely that which will build us up and not tear us down. Our thoughts affect our attitudes. As a result, you should take regular inventory of your thoughts and ask yourself: 'What have I been thinking about?' Spend time examining your thought life, as Satan deceives believers in their thinking. Many believers are of the opinion that the source of their misery or trouble is due to what is happening around them (their circumstances), when in fact it is due to what is happening on the inside of them (their thoughts).

Our minds are not born-again with the New Birth experience; they have to be renewed (Rom. 12:2). This renewing of our mind is a gradual process. Have you ever tried to banish a wrong thought that came into your mind, only for it to come right back? Satan will aggressively fight against the renewal of your mind. When a believer receives Jesus as their personal saviour, the Holy Spirit comes to dwell in them. The Bible teaches us that as a man knows his own spirit, and in so doing is the only one who knows his thoughts, so the Holy Spirit is the only one who knows the mind of God (1 Cor. 2:11). Consequently, a function of the Holy Spirit is to make known to us God's wisdom and reveal to us truths in His Word. This wisdom and revelation is imparted to our spirit, and our spirit then enlightens the eyes of our heart, which is our mind (Eph. 1:17-18). This happens so that we can understand on a practical level what is being ministered to us spiritually.

As believers, we are spiritual, and we are also natural. But the natural does not always understand the spiritual. Therefore it is vital that our natural minds are informed about what is going on in our spirit. However, when our mind is too busy, filled with reasoning, anxiety, worry, fear, our mind misses what our spirit is attempting to reveal through the Holy Spirit's enlightenment. Satan knows this fact, and he attacks our mind, waging war against us in our mind. He overloads and overworks our mind by filling it with every kind of wrong thought so it cannot be free and available for the Holy Spirit to work through our spirit.

Rom. 12:2 shows us that our actions will not change until our thoughts change. Right actions are the 'fruit' of right thinking. Many believers struggle trying to do this, but fruit is not the product of struggle. Fruit comes as a result of abiding in the vine (John 15:4), and abiding in the vine involves being obedient (John 15:10).

9.6 Authority of God's Word

Gal. 5:22 states that faith is a part of the fruit of the Spirit. It is through the reading of the Word of God and the enlightenment of the Holy Spirit that Christ in His fullness is known. The piece of armour known as the "sword of the Spirit" (Eph. 6:17) is the only piece of armour that has the ability to cut, wound, and hurt our enemy, the devil. It is not the Bible lying on our bedside table that makes the enemy flee, but rather the Word of God which is hidden in our heart, activated by the Holy Spirit, and spoken in appropriate situations.

We as believers must avail ourselves of God's Word by placing it in our heart, so that the Holy Spirit may bring it forth at the appropriate time to accomplish a complete and total victory. Have you ever seen a plant struggle to bring forth fruit? Have you ever heard a vine moan and groan and complain about how hard it is to produce grapes? Of course not! It is the nature of a vine to produce grapes. If the vine is protected and given nourishment, it will automatically produce fruit, unless it is starved or attacked by some outside force. So it is with the Christian; faith will automatically be the product of our abiding in the Word, which is Jesus (John 1:1; John 15:1-7).

Similarly, Jesus said in John 6:63 that "...the words that I speak to you are spirit, and they are life". The Word by itself does not make us free. It is the Word we know and speak that will deliver us (John 8:32). This is because the Word of God has authority, and it supersedes all authority of the Church, of reason, of intellect, and even of Satan himself. Speaking God's Word in faith brings the Holy Spirit into action, and it is He who wields this Word as it is spoken in faith. In Luke 4, when Jesus was tempted by the devil for forty days, it was the Word of God that Jesus used to defeat the enemy in the time of His temptation. Jesus constantly met His temptation by quoting from God's Word as He repeatedly stated the phrase "(I)t is written..."

9.7 Just Like Jesus

In all things, Jesus is our example. We are to place the same value on words as He did; words anointed and inspired by God. If Jesus places a high standard on the words that He speaks, then we need to be thoughtful about the words we speak, and make sure they contain peace, love, joy, and grace. Jesus said that He spoke only what He heard the Father speak (John 8:28-29).

In the New Testament we see the power that Jesus released and the miracles He performed through the words He spoke. Almost every recorded miracle Jesus performed was accomplished through His words. For example, at the wedding in

Cana, it was His words that changed a natural circumstance to meet a need. The Bible tells us that Jesus said "(F)ill the waterpots with water...Draw some out now, and take it to the master of the feast...the master of the feast had tasted the water that was made wine..." (John 2:7-9). There is no mention in the Bible that Jesus prayed over the water to change, or even rallied a prayer meeting. He did nothing special other than to speak!

But we know that there was something special about the words Jesus spoke, and His mother recognised this too when she told the servants: "Whatever He says to you, do it" (John 2:5). Mary knew that Jesus' instructions had to be followed precisely in order for the miracle to occur. But take a minute to think about those servants...the wedding guests had run out of wine, the master of the feast probably instructed them to obtain more wine, and Jesus instructs them to fill several waterpots with water, draw some of this 'water' and present it to the master! Knowing that water placed into a waterpot was going to remain water, they must have been so afraid of reprisal. Yet, they obeyed Jesus when He told them to draw some of this 'water' and present it to the master of the feast. How much more then should we, being the Body of Christ, value and obey Jesus' words?

At this point I would like to advise you not to begin analysing the kind of wine Jesus made, namely whether or not it contained alcohol, nor get caught up in needless controversy about this wine, and get distracted from the miracle that occurred. Knowing the alcoholic content of this wine will not help you, and it will not bring you any real understanding of the miracle that Jesus performed at this wedding. Focus on the miracle Jesus performed and get a grasp of the interaction between Jesus' words and the obedience to those words. The faith that you bring together from this passage can cause a change in your heart and in your life!

9.8 Hardness of Heart

In the story about Jesus walking on the water towards His

disciples (Mark 6:45-52), we read "(F)or they had not understood about the loaves, because their heart was hardened". The cause for the disciples' hearts to be hard was not due to sin, but because their focus was on things other than the miracle Jesus had just performed. Earlier in the day they witnessed Jesus taking five small loaves of bread and two small fish, and feeding an entire multitude of people. But now they were too occupied with trying to save their lives in the midst of a storm.

As a result, when they saw Jesus walking on the water, they were shocked or surprised to see Him. Having seen the miraculous power of God manifest itself a few hours before, they should have expected to see a miracle such as Jesus walking on the water if they had kept their minds stayed on that miracle, and continued thinking spiritually instead of naturally.

Again, in Mark 8:17-18, we read that Jesus was speaking to His disciples about the characteristics of a hard heart; "Jesus...said to them, 'Why do you reason because you have no bread? Do you not yet perceive nor understand? Is your heart still hardened? Having eyes, do you not see? And having ears, do you not hear? And do you not remember?'" In this passage of scripture Jesus gave us the indicators that are expressive of a hardened heart, namely: the inability to perceive, understand, see, hear, and remember whatever it is their heart is hardened towards.

A hard heart can be distinguished by an inability to understand what God is trying to show us, as we struggle to both grasp His spiritual truths in a way that we can apply to our lives, and hear His voice speaking to us. A hardened heart is not only caused by living a sinful life, but it can also be a result of being too focussed on everyday life, and what that involves. We become too reliant on our carnal senses, as demonstrated in Mark 9:17-28 when the disciples were unable to heal a boy with an evil spirit due to their thoughts being dominated by what they saw and experienced through the revelation of the evil spirit. The disciples could not perceive or understand spiritual truths. Although they may have been able to comprehend intellectually what they saw and heard, they did not engage these supernatural manifestations of God at a heart level and therefore did not apply these truths in their own lives, and in so doing influence their behaviour.

For example, if I were to ask you to quote a scripture relating to provision and prosperity, you may cite Deut. 28:8, 2 Cor. 8:9, Phil. 4:19, and so forth. Yet many believers still have lack. Does this then mean that God's Word is void of power or impossible of fulfilment? Of course not, there is no circumstance that God's Word cannot prevail over; nor is there a problem in your life that God's Word cannot surmount. However, if I had to ask you about your favourite sports team, clothes designer, or artist, many of these same believers could probably provide me with a wealth of information regarding goals scored, number of appearances, latest shoe trends, artistic interpretations, and the like. Whatever you focus on, that will dominate you.

Look again at Mark 6, where we started. In verse 52 it says that the disciples were hard-hearted "(F)or they had not understood about the loaves". The reason for their hard heart was not sin; they had not been in rebellion toward God, neither did they have pornographic magazines with them on the boat, nor were they drunk. Rather, their hearts were hardened towards God because they had not considered the miracle of the loaves. They neglected what God had done in their presence, and therefore did not give it priority in their lives.

If we were not so dominated by what is happening around us, we will not be amazed by supernatural occurrences. We should expect to see the miraculous power of God manifest in our lives all the time. But the benefit of understanding what causes a hardened heart is that we can reverse this process and use it to become hardened against the devil. If all you did was meditate on God's Word day and night, then you would make your way prosperous and have good success. There is no alternative. It does not take huge faith, but it does take pure faith.

We need to be sensitive to God, and we do that by the things we consider, being what we focus our attention on. Every person who has been greatly used of God was a fanatic in the matter of being separated from the world. You can love God and be carnal, but it will cost you your effectiveness. God's grace is always consistent, and His love towards you never changes. But when you consider something other than Jesus, you deaden yourself to the voice of God. It is not sin to have in-depth knowledge of your favourite sports team, clothes designer, or artist, but you will not miss anything by not knowing that information.

Putting God first may cost you your time, convenience, and some pleasures; but it will also cost you your strife, sickness, carnality, lack – all the things that are destroying your life and making you depressed, frustrated, and ineffective.

9.9 Anointing on Jesus

In order for us to follow Jesus' example of speaking words anointed and inspired by God, we need to understand how He did it. Many believers are of the opinion that Jesus' words carried such authority and power because He is the Son of God. Although Jesus is, has always been, and will always be the Son of God, while He carried out His earthly ministry, Jesus did not do all those mighty deeds on the earth as the Son of God. The Bible says that He voluntarily laid aside His power and glory as the Son of God (Phil. 2:6-8), and ministered as a man *filled and anointed with the Holy Spirit* (Acts 10:38). It was the anointing of the Holy Spirit that made Jesus' words so full of power and ability and which gave His words that quality to be able to perform the miraculous and change people's lives for the glory of God.

I agree that Jesus came to this earth to fulfil God's promises to mankind, but Jesus never began His ministry until after He was anointed by the Holy Spirit. Although Jesus had a divine nature when He was on this earth, He was also the Son of Man with a human nature. Jesus spoke with such authority and power because they were anointed and inspired by God through the Holy Spirit. When you live with the Holy Spirit having total influence in your life, you will abide in the anointing of God. The Holy Spirit dominated Jesus' life because He lived and walked in the Spirit. The results of a lifestyle dominated by the Spirit of God is found in Acts 10:38: "...God anointed Jesus...with power, who went about doing good and healing all who were oppressed by the devil..."

Also, looking at Jesus' life for a moment, we can see that He maintained the anointing that was on His life by frequently spending private time in prayer with the Father. Jesus was constantly abiding in the Father's presence in order to maintain the anointing on His life and ministry (Matt. 14:23; Matt. 26:36; Luke 6:12).

9.10 Releasing the Power in Our Words

At His ascension, Jesus gave that same power and authority to us, the Body of Christ. In Mark 16:17-18 Jesus says "...these signs will follow those who believe: In My name they will cast out demons; they will speak with new tongues; they will take up serpents; and if they drink anything deadly, it will by no means hurt them; they will lay hands on the sick, and they will recover". This is one of the greatest messages that the Church needs to hear, at a time such as this we possess, through Jesus, the ability to speak words anointed and inspired by God!

The ability to speak words so full of power and authority is that we can set this world on fire with the news that Jesus Christ has come to seek and to save all that are lost, and set men and women free from the power of the enemy. Satan has to bow his knee to the name of Jesus (Phil. 2:9-11). The Word of God spoken by believers will set in motion mighty wonders for the benefit of all mankind.

Every believer has the blood-bought right to speak boldly God's Word, words that are anointed, that can bring about miraculous results of life and liberty, set those enslaved to Satan free from bondage, and that accomplish whatever they are sent to do. Psa. 119:130 tells us "The entrance of Your words gives light; It gives understanding to the simple". God's Word spoken with the anointing of the Holy Spirit will be irresistible to the men and women of this world whose eyes have been blinded to the glorious light of the Gospel. Of course, I realise that God has given us a free will and the right to choose, but God's Word is a light to our path (Psa. 119:105). Once the seed of God's Word has been placed in the hearts of those men and women, the Holy Spirit will begin to convict them of the single sin of not receiving Jesus as their Saviour (John 16:8-9).

9.11 Meditating on God's Word

As I mentioned earlier, Jesus maintained the anointing that was on His life and ministry by constantly abiding in the Father's presence. Likewise, we are to continually recharge ourselves through prayer and meditation (Psa. 1:2; Jude 1:20). Many believers neglect to keep in close enough communication and fellowship with God. Consequently, their prayers become ineffective and their words seem powerless. But the anointing of God never leaves us, because He promised to never leave us nor forsake us (Heb. 13:5). In order to be used mightily of God, we must keep on fire the anointing of God in our lives; and we do this by meditating on the Word of God and by living a life of prayer and dedication to God (refer to Chapter 8 for more on living a life of prayer).

It is not enough to hear the Word of God; we need to meditate on it. We meditate on the Word of God by taking hold of the verse that has significance for us, memorise it and then begin to mutter it under our breathe; and as we go about with a daily routine, we should regurgitate that verse and mutter it under our breathe. Let us take 2 Tim. 1:7 as an example of what I mean with meditating on the Word:

"For God has not given us a spirit of fear, but of power and of love and of a sound mind"

I will mutter and repeat to myself: God has not...He has not...God has not..., then once I feel that my mind understands and has aligned itself with the Word of God, I move onto the next section of the verse: God has not given me a spirit of fear...I do have a spirit of fear...I am not fearful... God has not given me a spirit of fear..., and so I will continue until I have worked through the verse and as I said before, until once I feel that my mind understands and has aligned itself with the Word of God. Once your mind begins to understand and aligns itself with the Word of God, your spirit and soul (namely our personality, being our mind, our will, our emotions, and our conscience) will connect and a supernatural flow of the life of God from our spirit into our soul will take place.

Meditating day and night on God's Word is the key to thriving, flourishing and seeing the blessing of God in all that we set our hands to do. Begin to experience greater health, peace, stability and unceasing fruitfulness as you meditate on the Lord's wonderful promises for you today!

Receive Jesus as Your Saviour

Choosing to receive Jesus Christ as your Lord and Saviour is the most important decision you will ever make!

God's Word promises, "...that if you confess with your mouth the Lord Jesus and believe in your heart that God has raised Him from the dead, you will be saved. For with the heart one believes unto righteousness, and with the mouth confession is made unto salvation.... For "whoever calls on the name of the Lord shall be saved" (Rom. 10:9–10, 13).

By His grace, God has already done everything to provide salvation. Your part is simply to believe and receive. Pray out loud:

Jesus, I confess that You are my Lord and Saviour.

I believe in my heart that God raised You from the dead. By faith in Your Word, I receive salvation now.

Thank You for saving me!

Referring to Jesus as 'Lord' means you acknowledge Him as the owner, master, and king of your life. This is a total commitment. The very moment you commit your life to Jesus Christ, the truth of His Word instantly comes to pass in your now born-again spirit. You are now a brand-new you!

Receive the Holy Spirit

As His child, your heavenly Father wants to give you the supernatural power you need to live this new life.

The Bible says "For everyone who asks receives, and he who seeks finds, and to him who knocks it will be opened... If you then...know how to give good gifts to your children, how much more will your heavenly Father give the Holy Spirit to those who ask Him!" (Luke 11:10, 13). All you have to do is ask, believe, and receive! Pray out loud:

Father, I recognise my need for Your power to live this new life. Please fill me with Your Holy Spirit. By faith, I receive Him right now! Thank You for baptising me.

Holy Spirit, You are welcome in my life.

Congratulations! You are filled with God's supernatural power. Some syllables from a language you do not recognise will rise up from your heart to your mouth. (1 Cor. 14:14). As you speak them out loud by faith, you will be releasing God's power from within and building yourself up in the Spirit (1 Cor. 14:4). You can do this whenever and wherever you like.

It does not matter whether you felt anything or not when you prayed to receive the Lord and His Spirit. If you believe in your heart that you received, then God's Word promises you did. According to Mark 11:24 which says "Therefore I say to you, whatever things you ask when you pray, believe that you receive them, and you will have them". God always honours His Word!

Circle Books

Circle is a symbol of infinity and unity. It's part of a growing list of imprints, including o-books.net and zero-books.net.

Circle Books aims to publish books in Christian spirituality that are fresh, accessible, and stimulating.

Our books are available in all good English language bookstores worldwide. If you can't find the book on the shelves, then ask your bookstore to order it for you, quoting the ISBN and title. Or, you can order online—all major online retail sites carry our titles.

To see our list of titles, please view www.Circle-Books.com, growing by 80 titles per year.

Authors can learn more about our proposal process by going to our website and clicking on Your Company > Submissions.

We define Christian spirituality as the relationship between the self and its sense of the transcendent or sacred, which issues in literary and artistic expression, community, social activism, and practices. A wide range of disciplines within the field of religious studies can be called upon, including history, narrative studies, philosophy, theology, sociology, and psychology. Interfaith in approach, Circle Books fosters creative dialogue with non-Christian traditions.

And tune into MySpiritRadio.com for our book review radio show, hosted by June-Elleni Laine, where you can listen to authors discussing their books.

MySpiritRadio